Fifty Economic Fallacies Exposed

Fifty Economic Fallacies Exposed

Second edition

GEOFFREY E. WOOD

To Brian Carrie,
I hope it entertains,
and I trust it informs?
Best wishes,

Geoffrey Wood

iea
The Institute of Economic Affairs

Second edition published in Great Britain in 2014 by
The Institute of Economic Affairs
2 Lord North Street
Westminster
London SW1P 3LB
in association with London Publishing Partnership Ltd
www.londonpublishingpartnership.co.uk

First edition published in 2002 by
The Institute of Economic Affairs
in association with Profile Books Ltd

The mission of the Institute of Economic Affairs is to improve understanding of the fundamental institutions of a free society by analysing and expounding the role of markets in solving economic and social problems.

A CIP catalogue record for this book is available from the British Library.

ISBN 978-0-255-36695-3

Many IEA publications are translated into languages other than English or are reprinted. Permission to translate or to reprint should be sought from the Director General at the address above.

Typeset in Kepler by T&T Productions Ltd
www.tandtproductions.com

Printed and bound in Great Britain by Page Bros

CONTENTS

THE AUTHOR

Geoffrey Wood is Emeritus Professor of Economics at City University Business School, London, and Emeritus Professor of Monetary Economics at the University of Buckingham. He has also taught at the University of Warwick, and been on the research staff of the Bank of England and the Federal Reserve Bank of St Louis. He has published extensively in the areas of monetary economics and international economics. Among these publications are *Too Much Money?*, with Gordon Pepper (IEA, 1975); *Independence for the Bank of England?*, with Forrest Capie and Terry Mills (IEA, 1993); *The Right Road to Monetary Union Revisited*, with John Chown and Max Beber (IEA, 1994); and *Money Over Two Centuries: Selected Topics in British Monetary History* (Oxford University Press, 2012), comprising work with Forrest Capie and others, written over a period of some twenty years. His recent research has been on central bank independence and on regulation. He is a member of the Academic Advisory Council of the Institute of Economic Affairs and a trustee of the Wincott Foundation.

FOREWORD

It is often said that economics is applied common sense. Unfortunately, as I remember the man who owned the local bicycle shop saying to me when I was a child, 'the problem with common sense is that it is not common enough'. And so it is that the demand for this monograph by Geoffrey Wood, *Fifty Economic Fallacies Exposed*, never seems to decrease.

I was delighted that Professor Wood agreed to update this publication to allow the IEA to publish a new edition. A few old fallacies have been removed to make room for new ones (though, no doubt, the old ones will become relevant again in the future). But, as the author said to me, all the fallacies are essentially the same. They arise from an inability of people to understand supply and demand (and, by implication, opportunity cost).

Henry Simons once said: 'Economics is primarily useful, both to the student and to the political leader, as a prophylactic against popular fallacies.' Through the vehicle of undermining fallacies, Professor Wood brings to his audience good economics. As such, this new edition of *Fifty Economic Fallacies Exposed* is an important contribution to the IEA's educational mission.

The views expressed in this monograph are, as in all IEA publications, those of the author and not those of the

Institute (which has no corporate view), its managing trustees, Academic Advisory Council members or senior staff. With some exceptions, such as with the publication of lectures, all IEA monographs are blind peer-reviewed by at least two academics or researchers who are experts in the field.

PHILIP BOOTH

Editorial and Programme Director
Institute of Economic Affairs
Professor of Insurance and Risk Management
Cass Business School, City University, London

July 2014

ACKNOWLEDGEMENTS

I am indebted to the late Arthur Seldon, who was Editor of *Economic Affairs* when I first proposed a regular feature exposing economic fallacies, both for accepting my suggestion and for his ever useful editorial advice. Second, many thanks go to his successor, Colin Robinson, for continuing the feature and for his most helpful suggestions of fallacies to expose and of improvements to what I had written. Third, my colleague Forrest Capie deserves thanks for over the years drawing to my attention a good number of fallacies to discuss, and giving very useful comments on drafts. Fourth, and most important, my thanks go to my assistant Debra Durston. Mrs Durston worked with me for over 25 years with continual efficiency and unshakable good humour. Her contribution to all my work over the years has been considerable. I am particularly glad to be able to acknowledge it here, in a book to which, by her calmness under pressure, she has contributed so much.

Thanks are also due to Joe Little, of the University of Bristol, who helped with the selection of fallacies to be included in this revised edition.

INTRODUCTION

Each of the short essays in this volume comprises the application of basic economic analysis and logic to a frequently repeated but fallacious belief about one aspect or another of the economy. Occasional reference is made to an item of data, but that is always simply to illustrate a point; the argument never depends on data, but always on logic.

The essays aim to serve two purposes – to illustrate aspects of economic reasoning, and to expose wrong, occasionally counterproductively or even dangerously wrong, arguments. The topics are drawn from both micro-economics and macro-economics. But in every case the reasoning applied to them is either explicitly micro-economic or clearly derived from micro-economics. This reflects the fact that micro-economics, the analysis of firms and individuals interacting in markets, is the basis of *all* economic analysis.

PART 1

REGULATION AND MARKETS

TICKET TOUTS ARE HARMFUL AND WICKED. THEY SHOULD BE STAMPED OUT BY LAW

There is an idea about that being a ticket tout is in some unexplained way disreputable, and that those who deal with them, whether buying or selling, are disgracing themselves and their associates. One cannot refute a moral judgement by logic. It is not a matter of economics. But what economics can do is to show that ticket touts are useful, and that they provide a service to both seller and buyer. There is absolutely no case for making their activities illegal.

To see this, think about what a ticket tout does. And just for the moment, we shall not call what he trades in 'tickets' – we shall call them 'the item'.

Some person has a supply of the item surplus to what he wants. The item does not keep for ever – indeed, after a certain date it becomes useless. He can do several things with it – give it away, not use it (and thus let it go to waste), or he can sell it. If he wants to sell it, there are many methods open to him; but a very convenient one is to find someone who deals in the item, and is willing to buy it with the aim of reselling it, but bearing the risk that he may fail. The original possessor of the item, who is not a professional dealer, is willing to sell for a little less than he might receive from the final consumer in return for someone else bearing the risk of not selling the item.

The intermediary now has a stock of them, which he tries to sell. He tries to sell at a price higher than he paid, to people who want to buy it.

Now consider the whole transaction. One person had some items surplus to his wants. He sells them to someone who then tries to sell them to a person who does want to use them. No one has been harmed by the chain of transactions – and that is fortunate, for there are millions of such transactions every day. A newsagent buys newspapers and sells them on. A grocer buys food and sells it on. A dealer in government securities buys them and sells them on. We don't attach the discreditable name of 'tout' to newsagents, grocers and bond dealers and say their activities should be made illegal. Why do we do it to dealers in tickets?

If we banned ticket touts, we would be making both buyers and sellers worse off. And by making illegal a harmless activity which benefits all who take part in it, it would divert police effort away from dealing with real crime. The idea that ticket touts should be banned is nonsense.

June 1989

THE CONDUCT OF AN INDUSTRY – IN PARTICULAR, HOW IT SERVES CONSUMERS – IS IMPROVED BY GOVERNMENT REGULATION

It is widely believed that government intervention in industry can and does benefit consumers. Economists have developed careful and clear analyses of the situations when regulation could be desirable. But does regulation in practice have these desirable effects?

Adam Smith certainly doubted its efficiency. To restrain people from entering into voluntary transactions 'Is a manifest violation of that natural liberty which it is the proper business of law not to infringe but to support'. Nevertheless, he argued, 'those exertions of the natural liberty of a few individuals which might endanger the security of the whole society, are, and ought to be, restrained by the laws of all governments...' He defended regulation in such cases in principle. But he objected to the practice. The legislature, he argued, is directed not by a view of the common good, but 'the clamorous importunity of special interests'. His view was that whatever regulation could do in theory, in practice it usually benefits those regulated.

What does the evidence say? A pioneer in this area was George Stigler. In a study of the electricity industry in the

US, he found that regulation affected neither rates charged to customers nor profits earned for shareholders. In a study of the securities industry, he found that regulation governing the listing of new securities, presumably intended to protect the investor, had no significant effect on the returns to new shares as compared to ones already in the market.

A current UK example which should lead one to wonder about the benefits of regulation is food. When it was feared that eggs were likely to be harmful, and sales dropped, egg farmers were offered compensation – which was paid of course by a levy on consumers, who had just very plainly indicated in the market that they did not wish to support egg farmers! In contrast, how was a different group, one not close or important to the regulators, treated? Producers of non-pasteurised cheeses – a tiny group of farmers – and foreign cheese makers, were both threatened with having their products banned on health grounds before consumers had a chance to show if they were concerned!

Regulation has two vices. It restricts competition – all producers are compelled to behave in a similar way. And it restricts information – information has to go to the regulator, but not to the consumers who buy the product. Informed choice is not possible without information; and restricting competition means that there is less pressure to raise quality and lower cost. For these reasons, regulation by government generally harms the consumer. The best regulation is by competition combined with provision of information.

August 1989

THE STATE SHOULD STEP IN TO PROTECT THE ENVIRONMENT

There is now widespread popular concern about the 'quality of life' and the environment. Both are said to be deteriorating and, it is claimed, this can be stopped only by the state preventing destructive private actions which have no regard for the consequences for people. We need, it is said, planning to protect the world.

This is in many cases the opposite of the truth. It is state action that is the destroyer, private the preserver.

Two examples are useful. Consider the proposed High Speed 2 rail link. Even in its revised form this will be destructive of how people want to live. That is not a private action. It is the result of the state giving a body – High Speed 2 Ltd – the right to dispossess people of something at a price below that which would induce them to move voluntarily.

Town planning is another example. Buildings can be put up when permission is given – regardless of the wishes of those who live nearby – at the whim of a civil servant or the vote-catching urge of a politician.[1]

---

1   A colleague of mine has been sufficiently unfortunate to suffer both types of damage. Present HS2 plans threaten the foundations

Both these problems arise because politicians either take away property rights or refuse to acknowledge their existence. If people have rights in property – if they own it – they will preserve it.

Consider the above two examples. If people had to be paid to leave their homes or tolerate a train near their garden, the costs to society of building the rail link would be taken into account. If owners of houses were entitled to compensation for a hideous new building increasing congestion around them, again the cost of the building would be taken into full account.

This would produce efficient resource allocation; costs would be taken fully into account. And it would also produce the desired amount of preservation. Not, no doubt, everyone's desired amount – too much for some, too little for others. But it would produce what people were willing to pay for.

Acknowledging property rights in the environment would thus serve two purposes. More efficient resource allocation would take place. And the present debate about preserving the environment would be clarified. At the moment people call for preservation unthinkingly because the costs do not fall on them. If the cost of resisting a development was not being paid a large sum in compensation, then the objectors would think. As it is, they might as well resist.

---

of his house, and a building two streets away has blocked a fine view from his study.

Acknowledging property rights in the environment would preserve what people want. Not acknowledging these rights, having state planning, leaves the present and future environment up to the accidents of election timing and chance.

December 1989
(Updated April 2014)

FIRMS SHOULD NOT MAKE PROFITS

There seems to be an idea about that firms should not make profits. Railway companies are criticised for making profits. That a company which aimed not to make profits did not win the first franchise to run Britain's national lottery was thought by some to be undesirable, even disgraceful. Utility companies are condemned for making profits. But all this barrage of criticism is based on a fundamental misunderstanding; profits are a useful, indeed essential, part of an economy.

To see this, start with the example of a hypothetical firm. This firm makes and sells a good, shoes say. To make these goods it needs workers, leather and machines. And all three have to be paid for. The workers need to be paid their wages, salaries and benefits. The suppliers of leather have to be paid or they will take their cows elsewhere. And what about the machines? They do not have to be paid. But they did have to be bought, and, when they wear out, they will have to be replaced if the firm wishes to continue in business.

The firm could get the money to buy the machines in one of two ways (or a combination of them). It could borrow the money, or it could spend money that it had earned and saved in the past. If the money is borrowed, the lenders need to be paid. And if the firm uses its own funds, it is giving up the chance of lending the money to someone else. So either way, a return on the investment should be earned. True, it could fail to earn a return. Then, if the firm had borrowed the money, the firm would be closed down by its creditors trying to get back what they had lent, so it would not continue in operation. If it had used its own funds it would not face that risk; but, when the machinery wore out, the firm would not be able to continue in business without getting funds from someone else, for it would not have been earning anything to set aside for the future.

Now, what is that part of the firm's earnings that goes to pay for its capital? The answer is, profit. Profit, in other words, is a part of firms' costs just as wages are. Profits, like wages, are earnings which are essential for producing the firm's output.

Now, some organisations really do survive without making profits. The Institute of Economic Affairs is one. Like all such organisations the IEA depends on gifts. In the IEA's case, these gifts cover not just the capital costs, but a good portion of other costs, as well, but that is beside the main point. Organisations which choose not to make profits can and do survive, but they depend on the receipt of gifts.

At the other extreme, there are firms which are claimed to make 'excess profits'. One might think of 'excess profits' as being a rate of profit greater than necessary to keep the firm and its capital stock going year after year. Now, that has to be complicated a bit. If a firm is producing something for which there is unexpectedly strong demand, then it could earn 'excess profits' in the above sense for a time, until either the firm had expanded or other firms had entered the same line of business.

In general, 'excess profits' are eliminated by one of these routes, and are purely a transitory phenomenon, unless there is absence of competitive pressures, so that there is neither new entry, nor pressure to expand so as to prevent new entry, to the industry.

The main case in which 'excess profits' can be sustained is when government prevents other firms entering – when it creates a monopoly. Sometimes it regulates monopolies it has not created; and then its objective is to ensure that the excess profits are eliminated. But not, it is essential to emphasise, to eliminate the profits. If it did the latter, it would quickly eliminate the firm.

It is now almost possible to conclude. But before doing so, it is useful to touch on organisations which are 'not-for-profit'. Such organisations can have a wide range of objectives, and can take a wide range of forms. Some are, like the IEA, run as charities, and supported primarily by donations. They supply something regardless of whether it is paid for. Other organisations may cover their costs, but do not necessarily behave in other ways like profit-making firms. They may, for example, not raise their prices if there is excess demand for their goods. This does, of course, mean that they cannot raise the funds to allow them to expand so as to satisfy this demand, but presumably they have some other objective. But even in this case, they have to cover the costs of their capital, or they go out of business.

They do earn profits. They do not, however, respond to the signals to expand (or contract) that changes in profits provide.

To conclude, profits play an essential part in economic life. They represent the return on a firm's capital. Organisations can be 'not for profit'. In that case, they are either charities (whether in the strict legal sense or not) or earn profits but are not guided by them so as to vary the scale of their output. Apart from charities, it makes no more sense for a firm not to earn profits than it does for it not to pay its workers' wages.

In short, the current fashionable love of 'non-profit' firms is based on not understanding the nature and importance of profits. One can only hope the fad does not persist.

December 2000

PART 2

INTERNATIONAL TRADE AND FINANCE

ONE COUNTRY SHOULD NOT CUT ITS
TARIFFS UNLESS OTHERS DO

A common claim is that tariff reduction, perhaps even to the extent of moving to completely free trade, has to be reciprocal. One country it is said should not on its own adopt free trade. Some proponents of this recognise that unilateral free trade is beneficial, but use the promise of tariff reduction as a bargaining device to get other countries to reduce their tariffs. Some people claim that unilateral free trade is harmful. That is a fallacy, and one which can be very damaging.

If a country has no tariff barriers (or other barriers to international trade) it benefits in two ways. It benefits in consumption and it benefits in production.

The consumption benefits are the most obvious. Consumers can buy what they want wherever it is produced most cheaply, whether it is at home or abroad. There are not tariffs to make home-produced goods artificially cheap compared to those produced overseas; or, perhaps, to divert demand from the cheapest foreign supplier to one who, although more expensive, has from political favour won a lower tariff against his goods.

Consumers, in summary, can make the most of their income if they live in a country with no impediments to international trade. But of course consumers either are or depend on producers – to get the income they consume. Could free trade harm producers? The answer is that it could – and probably would harm some. But the economy as a whole would still gain. The reason is as follows. Producers are guided by the prices they see confronting them to produce what is most profitable for them and to do so as cheaply as they can. Prices thus direct resources to where they are most useful, as those producers to whom they are most valuable will pay most for them. If an economy is trading freely, without tariffs, its resources are making the most of the opportunities prescribed to them by the pattern of prices in the rest of the world.

The economy's resources will thus be used where it is most productive, relative to the rest of the world, for them to be. The economy will be making the most of the opportunities available to it. (These opportunities would of course be greater if all the world were a free trade area, but that is not really something any one country can produce.)

It is possible to construct a theoretical example where a country gains benefit by imposing tariffs, as these shift prices in its favour. But this example depends on the implausible assumption of great monopoly power and other countries not objecting and retaliating.

In summary, free trade is the best course a country can follow. Any other course impoverishes the country – by making production inefficient and denying consumers access to the cheapest markets. Protection is totally unjustifiable.

November 1991

FREE TRADE SHOULD BE FAIR

Visiting the United States, one is struck by a particular aspect of the discussions of free international trade. The USA is moving towards a North American Free Trade Agreement (NAFTA) which aims, in principle, to remove all government-created trade barriers to the movement of goods between the countries of that area – Canada, the USA, and Mexico. But a major hindrance has emerged – environmental standards in Mexico.

It is not clear whether those who raise this difficulty are concerned about the environment, or concerned just to maintain protectionism. For now, let us give them the benefit of the doubt. Let us assume that they really believe that efficient international trade requires the same environmental standards of every country which engages in it. That fallacy is the one exposed in this column.

Why do countries engage in international trade? One obvious reason residents of one country buy goods from residents of another is that they cannot be produced at home. By far the greatest part of international trade is trade which takes place because some goods can be produced better or more cheaply (or both) in one country rather than in another.

What produces these price differences? (I focus on price differences henceforth as they are what is at issue.) Climate is one factor. Another, very important, is relative abundance of resources, making some cheaper in one country than in another. Note that it is relative abundance in two senses – in one country as compared to another, and abundance produced by ample supply *relative to demand*. For prices to be low, there needs to be an abundant supply of a good relative to the demand for it. There being a lot of the good, or a little, in the physical sense does not give any information about price.

Now to NAFTA and environmental standards, where the above discussion will help clarify matters and expose the fallacy. Mexico can produce some goods more cheaply than the USA for a variety of reasons. Among these reasons, and particularly important for some heavy industries, is that manufacturers in Mexico do not have to meet the same low-pollution standards. Their 'smoke-stack industries' still have smoke stacks!

Why is this, and what would be the consequences of insisting that it be stopped before Mexico was allowed to export to the USA without any restrictions?

There are many reasons. Tastes vary. Smoke may be seen not as damaging to health, but as a symbol of thriving and prosperous industry. But one factor is almost certainly income. Lack of food and of clean water kills more rapidly than does a smoky atmosphere. People will buy food and clean water before worrying about clean air.

Suppose they were compelled to worry, and to do something about it. What would happen? Immediately, costs of production in Mexico would rise. Goods would be more expensive than before, and would either not be exported to the US or exported only in modest quantities, even if trade were free of impediments.

Well-being would be affected both in the US and in Mexico. US residents would not get some goods so cheaply and so would be worse off. Because they could not get these goods so cheaply, they could not afford to buy some other goods. The producers of such goods would be worse off, perhaps out of work. Meanwhile, some Mexicans would see the demand for their products disappear, and so they in turn could be unable to buy other goods, either from Mexico or elsewhere. In summary, both producers and consumers, in the USA and Mexico, would be made worse off if the Mexicans were not allowed to make use of some of their relatively abundant resources – cheap air, water and land. The policy makes no more sense than it would to say that, before the US is allowed to sell grain to Europe, it has to destroy the prairies.

What of the Mexican environment? Free trade between the US and Mexico will increase demand for all relatively cheap Mexican resources. Wages in Mexico will rise. And so will the value people put on clean air!

It is possible that environmental pollution will not diminish in Mexico. That would follow if Mexican tastes really were very different from those in other countries that have developed and become rich. In that unlikely event, it would not be grounds for preventing free trade – or at any rate no better grounds than it would be to prevent free trade with a country because its citizens wore brown shoes to the office.

Insisting that free trade requires similar environmental standards between countries before trade starts is equivalent to saying that all relative advantages should be extinguished by law before trade starts. Acting in accordance with that fallacy would be a recipe for poverty in all the prospective trading partners.

September 1993

FREE TRADE CAUSES UNEMPLOYMENT

Free trade has often been an unpopular policy. Various arguments have been advanced against it at various times in the past. The one that has resurfaced recently is that free trade – particularly between developed and less developed countries – will cause unemployment in the developed countries. (Interestingly, in the less developed countries fears about the consequences of trade with developed countries are sometimes voiced.)

In fact, it is not true that free trade causes unemployment. It may, however, have an effect on wages; this possibility is taken up below.

There are various reasons for engaging in foreign trade. Most obviously, one can buy goods not capable of being produced domestically. This comprises, when one thinks about it, rather a small group. Minerals, for example, may not be available. But beyond such categories, a lot can be produced if one does not mind the cost. Take the example of Scotland. That country – and Dundee in particular – is the world's leading producer of marmalade. Oranges are a crucial ingredient for that. They could be grown in Scotland – in hothouses; but they are not, because of the cost.

Cost differences account for a large part of international trade. People in one country buy from other countries goods which can be produced domestically, but only at a cost so high as to offset any saving in expenditure on transport.

There is a further reason for engaging in international trade.

Suppose that one country was less efficient than the rest of the world in producing *every* good. Less efficient in the sense that it required more units of everything used in production (that is, of every 'factor of production', to use the technical term) to produce every good in that country than it did elsewhere. Could that country engage in trade? Should it?

The answers are that it both could and should. It can do so by tending to specialise in the production of what it is least bad at. The reason is that, before trade opens up between this country and the rest of the world, prices within the country will be related to costs of production there. Hence the pattern of relative prices – the price of one good compared to others – will reflect these costs. This will also be true in the rest of the world. Therefore (except in an unusual special case, when *relative* costs of production are the same worldwide) relative prices before trade will be different in different countries. Now, where does that lead?

Suppose trade now opens up between countries. What will happen? People will see that relative prices differ in different countries, and will make their purchases accordingly. They will buy where goods are *relatively* cheaper. There will thus be two-way trade, even though one country has higher costs of production than the other. (The exchange rate will move so as to compensate for these production costs.)

The point is important, so an example may be helpful. Suppose in one country production costs are such that before trade the price ratio of two goods is 3:1; and in the other country, the ratio is 1:2. Then when trade opens up, consumers in the first country will wish to buy the first good overseas; and in the second country, they will wish to buy the second good overseas. Thus both countries take advantage of relative price differences produced by different production costs.

Each country will tend to specialise in the good which it is relatively more efficient at producing. And consumers in each country will gain, from a fall in the relative price of a good. But what about jobs?

It has so far been seen that trade can take place for three reasons, and that every one of these reasons leads to gains – in the form of either a wider choice of goods or a lower cost of some goods – for consumers.

These gains are, however, produced by a changing pattern of production. Within each economy, demand switches away from one good and towards the other (or others). What does this do to employment? Plainly it requires workers to move. It does not, however, put them completely out of a job. They are not wanted in one job but they *are* wanted in another – the same force which reduces demand for them in one activity increases demand in another. *The reduction and the increase in demand are inseparable.* Trade does cause workers to move – but it does not cause unemployment.

There are two qualifications to the above conclusion. First, unless workers can move instantaneously, neither requiring retraining nor having to look for work, there will be a *temporary* rise in unemployment. Second, if the workers cannot become qualified to work in the new jobs – whether through lack of ability or because there are barriers to acquiring the qualification (very long apprenticeships required by law, for example) – then they will, indeed, become unemployed. But aside from that particular case, free trade does not cause permanent unemployment. At worst, it causes a temporary rise in it.

Trade can certainly affect the pattern of earnings in one activity as compared to another, for it changes the pattern of demand for what produces these goods. Models can be constructed which give clear-cut predictions of the effect of trade on the distribution of income. But when the complexities of the world are introduced into the models, the predictions are not so clear-cut. Relative wages are changing all the time, and trade plays a part in producing these changes; but the size, and sometimes the direction, of the effect is seldom unambiguous.

Free trade does not cause unemployment. What it *does* do is change patterns of demand within economies. This leads to changed patterns of employment, and there can be transitional unemployment while adjustment to this new pattern is going on. Those who maintain that trade causes permanent unemployment, or that the temporary unemployment it causes should be resisted, are really saying that the pattern of demand for goods should never change. For it is these changes that require changes in the structure of output, and they require changes *regardless* of what has produced the change in the pattern of demand.

Trade is only one of the many factors that cause economic change. Abandoning free trade would not prevent economic change; it would only make people poorer, by restricting access to where goods are cheaper than at home. It is a recipe for poverty, and not even for poverty at high levels of employment.

June 1996

A CURRENT ACCOUNT DEFICIT IS A PROBLEM

Many commentators lament that Britain is running a deficit in the current account of the balance of payments. Some worry particularly about our deficit in goods – what is called the visible balance. The second concern is always misplaced. The first is slightly more complicated. It is therefore better to deal with the simple matter first.

International trade is basically of two *types* – trade in goods and trade in services. Exports of either generate foreign earnings, so, from that point of view, it does not matter what is exported. Indeed, it is perfectly normal as countries develop for them to produce and trade in services. International trade in services has been in recent years the fastest-growing part of such trade.

Some people worry because manufactured goods have become a smaller part of our output. That is a separate concern. But it is worth remarking that the arguments and evidence do not support the claim that it is intrinsically better to produce manufactured goods rather than services.[1]

---

1   An excellent review of these arguments is contained in N. F. R. Crafts's 1993 Hobart Paper, *Can De-industrialisation Seriously Damage Your Wealth?* London: Institute of Economic Affairs.

Given that the composition of exports does not matter, what about their total? Does it matter if we are exporting fewer goods and services than we are importing?

The best way to answer this question is to start with another. How are we paying for these goods and services? Some of them are paid for by our export earnings. Others are paid for in one of two ways – by running down our savings or by borrowing. Like an individual or a company, more can be spent than is earned, provided savings are reduced or borrowing increased. There are many circumstances where such action is perfectly sensible. There can be favourable investment opportunities, a temporary drop in income, or a chance to buy something more cheaply than usual. There is nothing wrong with borrowing; what matters is what it is for. If spending is wasteful, it is wasteful whether current income or borrowed funds are used.

The same is true for a country. If individual decisions by residents, whether firms or individuals, lead to a current account deficit, then a decision has been taken to spend more than income. If the funds being borrowed to finance that spending are used wisely, there is no problem. If they are not used wisely, then it is foolish spending, *not* the act of borrowing, that is the problem.

A striking example occurred in the United States. On average, that country ran a deficit on current account from the last quarter of the 19th century into the first decade of the 20th. It did so because there was a tremendous demand for funds to invest. Population, industry, and agriculture were all expanding westwards. The funds were lent from the residents of European countries, where the expected rate of return on investment was on average lower than in the United States. No one – at any rate, no one I know of – has claimed that the decline of the US set in with that foreign borrowing. It was used productively. The balance-of-payments deficit it engendered was in no way symptomatic of a problem.

Sometimes such deficits can be symptoms of problems (though not problems in themselves). For example, the symptom can be of 'excess demand'. Easy monetary policy may have over-stimulated demand, leading not just to rising prices, but also (as goods become harder to obtain or more expensive at home) to more purchases from abroad. If the exchange rate is floating, it will be driven down. And if it is pegged, there will be pressure to devalue.

Before summing up, one point remains. If a country is borrowing abroad, it is not necessarily increasing *net* overseas indebtedness. That may seem surprising – if a person borrows, his or her debts increase. But even in that case, if he or she has assets, they may be increasing in value more rapidly than the new debts. The same can be true of a country. The value of Britain's overseas assets has in recent years increased more rapidly than her overseas debts; increasing borrowing need not, and in this case did not, bring increased indebtedness.

Now to conclude. Overseas earnings are overseas earnings; it does not matter whether they come from the sale of goods or sale of services. A current account deficit is not itself a problem. It implies foreign borrowing. What matters is not the borrowing, but what has produced it and what it is being spent on. Current account imbalances are symptoms – but they can be symptoms of sensible decisions or of folly.

November 1993

THE COUNTRY SHOULD BE MORE COMPETITIVE

In an article published in the *Daily Mail* on 4 April 2014, David Cameron, Britain's Prime Minister, as well as saying a good few sensible things repeated a very foolish thing that has been said by many politicians (and others) in the past. He wrote, a sentiment many will share, 'I am frustrated by the hoops you have to jump through to get anything done.' But just before that, after a list of some of these 'hoops', he had written, 'The nations we are competing against don't stand for this kind of paralysis.'

This idea that we are in a competition with the rest of the world, and that we have to be better than them at everything, is nonsense despite the numerous references we see to 'Britain's overseas competitors'. This was shown by David Ricardo (the son of an immigrant, incidentally) over 150 years ago.

Countries can be rich or poor, efficient or inefficient, but they can always compete in world markets. They specialise according to what is known as *comparative advantage*. And 'comparative' is a key word. The following demonstration of the argument is essentially Ricardo's.

Start by imagining a country which is not open to the rest of the world. It does not engage at all in foreign trade.

But there is a market system inside that country. There is internal trade, between producers and consumers. The next point to observe is that there cannot be trade without there being prices. Prices are inevitably *established* by trade. There cannot be one without the other. (That may at first glance seem an odd thing to say. After all, we are accustomed to going in to shops and finding the prices already there. But these prices are set by the shopkeeper in the expectation of some trade pattern. If demand turned out differently from expected, prices would soon be changed.)

To summarise so far then, our imaginary economy, cut off from the rest of the world, has a fully developed set of relative prices (the prices of goods relative to other goods). Now imagine that the barriers between this imaginary country and the rest of the world vanish, and the citizens of this economy discover that relative prices are different overseas. For example, suppose that the internal prices were such that if you reduced your wine consumption by one bottle per year, you could with the money buy a pound of cheese. But you discover that overseas, the cheese you could buy if you gave up consuming a bottle of wine was only half a pound in weight. Cheese, in other words, was more expensive relative to wine abroad than it was at home.

What happens next? Foreigners would observe that by coming to this country and supplying wine, they could get more cheese than they could at home. For a bottle of wine would buy them a pound, not a half-pound of cheese. And residents of this country would also gain; for prices would adjust to reflect the increased demand for cheese, and they would end up with more wine than before and, if they wished, no less cheese.

Now residents of both countries have gained, and there has been no mention of how 'competitive' either economy is. We could now assume that to produce either good, either wine or cheese, our imaginary country which we started with required twice, or three times, or however many times we wished, the amount of inputs per unit of output as did the rest of the world. That does not matter. It does not prevent the economy engaging in, and gaining from, international trade.

Trade between countries is not a competition in which there are winners and losers. It is a mutually beneficial activity, from which both sides gain. (There is one special case. If, when a country opens up to trade, it finds that relative prices abroad are the same as they are at home, then there is no possibility of fruitful exchange. But there are no losses either. In that special case the country neither gains nor loses from trade.)

So, the notion that countries 'compete' with one another in international trade is totally misconceived. And not only misconceived. It can cause harm, if it leads to policies which impede international trade. If, for example, we start protecting firms by tariffs or subsidies to produce 'national champions' then we are wasting resources.

Nevertheless, that said, it is necessary to be fair to those who talk of national 'competition'. Obviously, it is better to be more productive rather than less. For the more productive one is, the better off one is. Some of the schemes to make us more 'competitive' are actually designed to make us more productive. And that is unequivocally a good thing.

So, to sum up. First, the idea that nations 'compete' with one another in international trade is totally misguided. It can lead to harmful policies. Countries gain by engaging in trade with the rest of the world. Trade is a mutually beneficial activity, not a competition. If policies justified by 'competitiveness' are actually intended to raise productivity, then they are aimed at a sensible goal. But they are more likely to be sensible if it is clear what they are for.

June 1997
(Updated April 2014)

INTEREST RATES AND EXCHANGE RATES

Despite the numerous problems of the euro zone, some people want to join the euro. Some businessmen want to do so because, they claim, it will boost exports. The Liberal Democrats want it because it is to them self-evidently a good thing to do. There is a desire to fix the exchange rate, and that is about all that is available to fix to. Some just like certainty, but others fear 'speculators'. For example, to quote one businessman a few years ago,

> We should join in EMU [Economic and Monetary Union] because we do not have the freedom to set our own interest rates. If we move them away from where speculators like, the currency is attacked.

The quotation paraphrases the remarks of a well-known businessman (and EMU enthusiast) in a recent interview. Whether or not Britain should join EMU is a question which involves many strands of argument, political and economic. But the idea that we cannot set our own interest rates outside EMU is fallacious, and has no place in a serious discussion of that complicated subject.

The claim is part of the body of beliefs which holds that countries have to protect themselves against multinational companies and speculators, forgetting that nations are made up of individuals, many of whom work for or own multinationals or firms which make a business out of for-eign-exchange speculation. But it is useful to consider the interest-rate claim separately, as it will no doubt be made with increasing frequency as EMU advances.

First, exchange rates do not always change when in-terest rates do. It depends on many factors – including whether the exchange-rate change was expected, what was happening to interest rates elsewhere, and, particu-larly relevant to the present discussion, why the interest rate changed.

So why do interest rates change? The answer is greatly influenced by the objective that monetary policy, usually conducted nowadays by the central bank varying a short-term interest rate, is trying to achieve. In an increasing number of countries, the objective of the policy is now to achieve and maintain a particular rate of inflation.

Given that the interest rate is set to achieve a target in-flation rate, suppose the interest rate is moved. Why might the exchange rate change? If the objective of monetary pol-icy is still the same rate of inflation as before (and nothing has changed overseas) then the exchange rate will change if the move has made the currency more attractive (or less) than before. Suppose the exchange rate appreciates. This means the currency has become more attractive. Either prospective buyers of the currency have become more convinced the inflation target will be achieved; or alterna-tively, there was never much doubt about that, but some-thing has happened to the domestic economy to require a higher interest rate to achieve the target. The first gives one confidence in the currency, the second increases the prospective return from holding it. Both make it more attractive, and thus tend to raise its price – to make it appreciate on the foreign exchanges.

Hence one complaint, when a currency appreciates and makes life harder for firms competing with firms elsewhere, is the result of policy to resist inflation. Would those who complain want higher inflation? They might say no, but they want fixed exchange rates. That is all very well, but fixed exchange rates are only satisfactory if, among other conditions, the inflation rate in the countries the rate is fixed to is acceptable. There can only be trivial inflation differences within a single currency area.

And what if rates are cut? The same argument applies. The currency will fall if holding it has become less attractive. But the rate cut takes place for a reason – either to ease up on inflation control, or because the same inflation can now be achieved with a lower interest rate.

To summarise, in general exchange rates move as a consequence of interest-rate changes in a way consistent with the consequences of that change for the domestic economy, and, very interestingly, in a way which helps to achieve those consequences. If, for example, the exchange rate appreciates, this helps slow inflation; and if it depreciates, this boosts demand for domestic goods, and makes inflation, at least for a time, higher than it would have been otherwise.

Exchange-rate movements in response to interest-rate changes are not irrational, based on whim. They are a conscious response to analysis of a policy change. That statement is, of course, a generalisation. Markets – like policy-makers – make mistakes, sometimes going too far or not far enough, and sometimes even in the wrong direction. But if they are wrong on average, then those who are making the mistakes lose money and go out of business. Markets make mistakes, but they are not – as the belief that we cannot control our own economic conditions except as part of a large currency bloc implies – consistently foolish, irrational or misguided.

That conclusion leads to an interesting puzzle. The businessman whose remarks were summarised at the start of this discussion was highly successful. Other, equally successful, businessmen have expressed similar views. They have achieved their success by skill, industry and the occasional bit of luck. None of them would say that the behaviour of the markets in which they worked, and thus their success in those markets, was entirely the result of chance and irrationality. So why do they think markets with which they are not familiar are dominated by such influences?

December 1998

BRITAIN'S ECONOMY SHOULD
BE BETTER BALANCED

At the time of writing (April 2014) the British economy seems to be growing quite strongly. But there are complaints (and not just from opposition politicians) that the recovery is 'unbalanced'.

Now, what can be meant by that? Some complain that there is a housing bubble developing. That is not easy to judge, but if true would be a matter for concern. Bubbles burst and can have harmful consequences beyond those directly involved. There are, though, three other concerns that are not so worth thinking seriously about, for they are simply fallacies, readily exposed as errors of reasoning.

Britain is not investing enough is one complaint; another is that we are not exporting enough; and the third is that exports are from too small a part of the economy.

The first two fallacies are covered in more detail on pages 113 and 28 of this book. To summarise: investment fluctuates very substantially over the business cycle, and anyway what matters is not how much is spent but how productive it is. And exports are not an end in themselves, but a means of obtaining foreign goods, and also part of the international flow of capital. An export surplus means we are lending abroad, a deficit that foreigners are net lenders to here. What follows from that is discussed on pages 28–31.

Now to the 'composition' of exports.

First think about an individual – the author, for example. I 'export' – that is, supply to other people – services in the form of economic speaking, writing and advice. I very seldom buy anything from these particular people, though. Rather I use what they pay me to buy other things: books, food, haircuts, plumbing services, for example. These are my 'imports'. Notice that my 'exports' are highly specialised – essentially one thing. My 'imports', in contrast, are highly diversified.

That is not at all surprising. However good (or bad) I may be at economics, I am better at that than I am at, say, cutting my own hair or plumbing my own house. I have, like almost everybody else in the world, specialised in what I am good at compared with the other things I could do. No one would suggest that I need to diversify my output, unless they had a low sense of humour and wanted to see the results of my cutting my own hair or wanted my house to be flooded.

Let's now look at a small country – New Zealand is a good example: big enough to be a real country, but with a population about half that of London. It may be geographically large, but it is economically small. Should that country diversify?

Some years ago, it did try. New Zealand imported all its motor cars. That's not really surprising; most people would be surprised if there were several car manufacturing plants in London in the business of supplying cars to London. The then government (of which Robert Muldoon was prime minister) decided that New Zealand should produce its own cars, so imposed very high taxes on car imports. The consequence was not the development of a thriving motor car industry. Rather what developed were a few small factories which assembled Japanese cars from imported kits. These cars differed in two ways from what had been imported previously: they rattled more and they were more expensive.

The policy was ended. Now of course there was nothing to stop New Zealand developing a car industry, just as there is nothing to stop me cutting my own hair – apart from New Zealand as a whole (and me) being better at something else, and better off by spending time doing it.

New Zealand and I are following the advice of the great David Ricardo, who getting on for 200 years ago developed the principle of comparative advantage. Put briefly it says that individuals, and countries, gain by specialising in what they can do relatively better than other people. Someone may be good at everything, someone else not very good at anything. But they can still trade with each other to mutual advantage by specialising in what they are best at and buying other things.

From that point of view, cries that Britain is overspecialised and that the economy is 'distorted' – From what, incidentally? What is its 'natural shape'? – are totally misguided. They are a recommendation that Britain make herself worse off.

Underlying that misguided recommendation there is a concern that could in principle be genuine. What if the market for the products of a major sector dried up suddenly, or just shrank a lot? This could happen to a country. It happened to Finland when the Soviet Union collapsed. The reason was not because Finland had specialised in only a few goods but because it had specialised in exporting to one country. Similarly, demand for Britain's financial sector could suddenly collapse. A possibility, but we should not forget that sector is only a part of a very large service sector. And further, if the demand for that collapsed, rather than declined slowly as the result of changes, say, in regulation overseas, then other sectors would seem unlikely to be totally unaffected.

To conclude, then, Britain's current growth could indeed be across a broader base. But that is always true. A conscious government policy of diversification would make Britain a poorer nation, and could bring benefits only under circumstances which are very unlikely to come about.

Claims that the economy, or its growth, is 'unbalanced' are often made. But however often they are made, that does not make them sensible.

April 2014

BRITAIN WOULD LOSE 3 MILLION JOBS BY LEAVING THE EU[1]

Many arguments are advanced over whether Britain should leave the EU or stay in. Most of these (apart from the purely emotional ones: 'We need to be part of "Europe"' or 'We should be free to govern ourselves') require careful evaluation of the facts on both sides. But the assertion that 'Britain would lose 3 million jobs by leaving the EU' is not one of them. It is based on a very old economic fallacy, one that is not just a failure of logic but one that is completely incompatible with all recorded history. Before discussing the fallacy in general terms, it is useful to deal with this specific example.

First we must set out the circumstances that are assumed for the purpose of this discussion. To make the case as favourable as is possible to the fallacy, we make the following assumptions. A decisive, unarguable, majority of British voters cast their votes in favour of leaving the EU. The next day, we leave. Britain reverts of course to a wide range of legal and institutional previous situations. And it

---

1 This 'fallacy exposed' is written before the referendum on Scottish independence. All the arguments would still hold. Only the name of the country discussed needs to be changed.

reverts to the same trading relationship with the EU as all other countries which are neither members nor in some form of association with it. What happens next?

Some firms would face higher tariffs than before when selling to customers in the EU. These firms would therefore face an immediate drop in demand for their goods. If they expected this to last, they would lay off labour. But other firms would almost simultaneously, and for the very same reason, face a rise in demand. These are the firms that produced goods in competition with firms that exported to Britain from the EU. Hence, due to the higher tariffs between Britain and the EU some firms would face a drop in demand and others a rise in demand.

These direct effects are far from the end of the chain of reactions to Britain's EU departure. People in Britain would start to look for substitutes for the previously (non-British) EU-sourced goods. Some of these would come from other countries – Australia, New Zealand and Chile could replace, for example, wines previously imported from continental Europe. (There might also be an increase in English wine production.) The demand created overseas by this increased British expenditure would raise incomes there, and these countries would undoubtedly spend some of this on goods from Britain. Why undoubtedly? Because they already do import from Britain – they already buy some British goods, and could now afford to buy more. Meanwhile, more substitutions would be taking place at home in Britain. British manufacturers would see gaps in the market that were previously filled by goods from the Continent, and would start to supply goods for these gaps, just as they have moved into gaps in the market in the past. But let's assume for a moment that all these changes lead to a net reduction in demand for British goods. What will happen then? Most likely, the net fall in demand for sterling to buy our exports will lead to the pound depreciating. Though the chain of events may be complex this will lead net exports and net imports to return roughly to where they were before.

So the fact that almost no workers are completely specialised, unable to do any job but one, will mean that there will not be '3 million jobs lost' should Britain leave the EU. These workers will move to other jobs. It is certainly true that these jobs will not necessarily pay as much as the previous ones. But then other forces come into play. Workers will start looking around for better jobs, firms will start seeking higher value products, and so forth. Indeed, every month the British economy creates and destroys hundreds of thousands of jobs as tastes change and new products are developed. From 2004 to 2011 the British economy was creating between 3 and 4 million new jobs every year – with old ones being destroyed. Leaving the EU would just add another, relatively small, twist to this process of job creation and destruction that is a natural part of any healthy economy.

And of course, most important of all, human wants are also not completely specialised. If we cannot get, say, French cars at the same price as before that does not mean that we will not buy any car. The same applies for all products. And further, and this takes us to the general fallacy embodied in the '3 million jobs lost' assertion: people's wants are not, or at any rate have not been so far in human history, finite. The richer people get, the more they want. They do not necessarily want more of the same thing either. Tastes develop and new wants are discovered. This, it has to be stressed, is natural, and not simply produced by advertising and therefore in the eyes of some undesirable. When I was a child I did not like opera – not because I did not like the opera I had heard, but simply because I did not really know it was there to like. As I grew older I discovered it and liked it. Tastes expand. And this expansion is a function of age and experience as much as income.

Many times it has been claimed that economic stagnation is inevitable because people have everything they want, or at least that it will become inevitable when all people have everything they want. We are yet to see that stagnation.

So to conclude: the idea that Britain will 'lose 3 million jobs' if there is a vote to leave the EU is just another example of an old fallacy – that human wants are finite. Of course, it also manages to include not just that old fallacy, enough on its own to destroy the claim, but also the belief that people can do only the job they are currently in, and are incapable of learning and changing.

It really is hard to believe that honest, serious, men can genuinely believe that Britain will 'lose 3 million jobs' by leaving the EU. There is plainly much educating still to be done. British workers are capable of learning and changing. It is to be hoped that those who make the lost jobs claim are as capable as British workers in general.

April 2014

GERMANY IS HARMING THE REST OF THE EURO ZONE BY EXPORTING SO MUCH

Germany keeps being told that it is a major beneficiary of the euro because it is exporting so much, and is indeed harming the rest of the euro zone by doing so. It must pay up to save the euro. But how much should Germany pay? No one seems to have thought about that.

There is though a more basic question. How much does it make sense for Germany to pay? What sort of bill would be reasonable? In fact the best approximation one can arrive at is a bill of zero.

Why zero? What about all the exports that have been produced as a result of the German currency being kept down by euro zone membership? These net exports are actually the problem for Germany.

Germany has been exporting more goods and services than it has been importing. So people in other countries have been making net transfers of funds to Germany. If they cannot earn these funds – and they did not because if they had Germany would not have run a trade surplus – they must have borrowed them. A trade surplus being run by a country means, in other words, that it is a net lender to at least part of the rest of the world, and in effect to the rest of the world as a whole.

That is certainly not always bad. Often it is good for both borrower and lender. A classic example is the lending by Britain to the United States that went on from just after 1870 to shortly before World War I. That lending was beneficial to both sides. In the US it was invested productively, developing and opening up the prairies. These were, and still are, some of the most productive agricultural land in the world. The investment helped to make the US a major and very prosperous agricultural producer. And Britain meanwhile not only earned a higher return on capital than could be earned by investing at home (Britain was even then a mature developed economy) but saw a sustained fall in the cost of living as food prices fell due to the imports that started to flow from the US.

Recent German investment has not all been like that. Some has been productive – motor car factories in Brazil, the Czech Republic and Mexico, for example. But much of it has just been lending to enable governments and individuals to consume more than they have been earning. As is now clear, many of the recipients of these loans are unable to pay them back. So in contrast to the earlier British/US experience, where both sides gained, both sides have lost.

Another aspect of this becomes apparent if we think about what would have happened in Germany if net exports had been smaller. Workers and factories would not have sat around. More goods and services would have been produced for investment and for consumption *inside*

Germany. By increased investment Germany would have become more productive. And because individuals in Germany could have consumed more they could have had a higher standard of living. These big exports have in effect been a subsidy from Germans to many of their trading partners.

That is not the end of the story, nor the end of the bad news for Germany. What an economy produces can be roughly divided into two categories: goods that are traded internationally and goods that are not. These categories – tradable and non-tradable goods as they are termed – are not of course clear cut, but some goods are much more easily traded internationally than others. The depressed German exchange rate has shifted productive resources, labour in particular, from the non-traded to the tradable sector. These resources are more productive there only so long as the exchange rate stays at its current artificial level. When that changes, they will have to incur all the costs of moving back. And, of course, they have been employed producing goods for which in many cases Germany may never be paid.

This is actually the exact reverse of what is now facing Australia. Its exchange rate has been driven up by a mineral boom. Policy makers and voters there are now thinking about two issues. What is a reasonable distribution of the benefits of the strong currency? And what planning should there be to deal with the inevitable end of the boom?

In conclusion, then, it is clearly wrong to say that Germany has benefited because of the boost to its exports delivered by a depressed euro. There have been some benefits, for some of the associated overseas investment has been more productive than it would have been at home; but there have also been some costs. The net effect is immensely difficult to calculate, but there can be no doubt that claims that Germany has gained so Germany must pay are just wrong.

These claims are yet another example of the widespread but fallacious belief that a trade surplus is in itself a good thing. Equally fallacious is the belief that a trade deficit is always a bad thing. There are inevitably associated capital flows with any trade imbalance, and what is done with them matters a lot.

April 2014

PART 3

INFLATION

RAISING INTEREST RATES CAUSES INFLATION

Over the past year the government has raised interest rates several times, with the aim of reducing inflation. This policy has come under attack by some who claim that far from reducing inflation, raising interest rates will increase it. This claim is a fallacy; and it is this claim we shall deal with here. It must be emphasised that it is only that aspect of criticism of the policy that is addressed – the present article is not concerned with whether the policy reduces inflation, whether it is the best way to reduce inflation, or whether rates have been raised too much or too little.

It is true as a matter of arithmetic that because the interest rate charged on mortgages is in the consumer price index, a rise in the mortgage rate raises inflation, and a fall lowers it. That does mean that if the mortgage rate were dropped from the index, and no other measure of housing costs put in its place, the index would undoubtedly be lower than it is now. But a measure of the cost of living which did not include housing costs would be a pretty poor measure. Some other figure to represent the cost of housing would have to be entered. That would be unlikely to move in steps as the mortgage rate does – so the time path of the consumer price index would be different – probably smoother. But there is nothing to say the index would be any lower; it could well be higher. So that argument for higher interest rates causing inflation is wrong.

There is also another argument. Higher interest rates, it is said, add to firms' costs, and also add to pressure for higher wages. That, it is claimed, is the route by which they cause inflation. The trouble with that argument is that it can be applied to any price. A rise in the price of bananas leaves people with less to spend on other things, just as a rise in interest rates does to those who are net borrowers. Hence one would say that a rise in the price of bananas leads to demand for higher wages, and leads to inflationary pressures. One could go through that argument about the price of every good in the economy. The conclusion would be that a rise in the price of any and every good is a cause of inflation, and thus conclude, not very helpfully, that the cause of inflation is rising prices!

The policy recommendation which follows from this conclusion is that it would be sufficient to prevent inflation that all price increases be forbidden. Notice *sufficient*: on the above argument, nothing else would be necessary! Conversely, cutting prices would reduce inflation! The folly is now at its most transparent. For that policy was tried in the UK; nationalised industries received increased subsidies to hold down prices in the 1970s. Inflation got worse, not better, as these subsidies were financed.

The claim that higher interest rates cause inflation is fallacious; and leads to conclusions and advice even more absurd than the claim itself.

February 1990

CREDIT CONTROLS ARE BETTER
THAN INTEREST RATES

As interest rates have been raised to reduce inflation, it has become increasingly asserted that credit controls would be better, in some way less painful, perhaps also better 'targeted'. These claims are confused. Indeed, they exemplify a failure to understand supply and demand analysis.

Interest rates are raised at times when demand exceeds supply. People are trying to borrow and spend more than others are saving, so the banks expand credit, thus adding to inflationary pressures. There can also be borrowing from overseas, which in these conditions puts downward pressure on the exchange rate and can thus add a once-for-all boost to prices. It seems appealingly simple to say, 'apply credit controls'. Even if these work (very doubtful nowadays) they are not painless or even less painful than interest rates. They are just different.

Existing borrowers do not face higher charges. The burden falls entirely on new borrowers – who cannot get funds at all. They face, in effect, an infinitely high price! It is as if instead of raising rates all round, rates were raised to new borrowers until none wanted to borrow. The idea that credit controls are painless is plainly absurd.

It is sometimes said that it is 'unfair' that existing borrowers have to face higher interest rates than at the start of their loans. This is of course a peculiar idea of fairness – that the burden should fall *entirely* on people who want to borrow after a certain date. And not only does the proposal embody a peculiar idea of fairness – it is also inefficient. It is inefficient in several ways.

First, the scheme is targeted purely according to when the loan is proposed. Second, and more important, it works only on borrowers – it does not work on savers. For the purpose of raising rates is to bring borrowing in line with desired savings. Raising saving can help achieve this end. Giving people an incentive to save more works on everyone – people who have not borrowed, existing borrowers and people who are planning to borrow. Credit controls work only on the last of the groups.

In summary, credit controls are not 'fairer' in how they allocate burdens than are higher interest rates. They are just different. With regard to efficiency, they are inferior. And all this is based on the assumption, to be discussed in the following 'Fallacy' (pages 60–62), that they can work in a modern open economy.

April 1990

CREDIT CONTROLS – DO THEY WORK?

In the previous 'economic fallacy exposed' it was shown that, contrary to popular claims, credit controls are not a painless way of restricting bank lending. Rather, they just impose pain on different groups from those which would suffer if bank lending was restricted by use of interest rates. That argument was conducted on the basis of assuming that credit controls are actually effective. This column shows that they (credit controls) are, in fact, totally ineffective except in circumstances which we certainly do not welcome.

It should first of all be observed that the evidence that they worked in the past is far from clear-cut. They were usually imposed at times when the economy was booming, and when demands for consumer goods had been growing rapidly. People do not keep adding to their stocks of those goods without limit. What they do is build up a stock of them, and, having done so, use that stock until it is time to replace it. In other words, the demand for consumer goods inevitably has a strong fluctuation to it.

Credit controls were imposed when the demand had been strong for some time, and thus approaching its peak. It was likely that these demands would turn down in any event. That is why it is far from clear that the controls actually worked. But that is not the argument here. This column argues that simply on the grounds of logic such controls can no longer have any significant effect. Suppose that credit controls are imposed. The consequence is initially that some people are denied access to credit and interest rates are lower than they would otherwise be. What happens next? People, including the suppliers of credit, attempt to evade these controls. What means can be used to do so?

An obvious method is to go outside the jurisdiction of those who have imposed the controls – in the present case to go to a foreign country, for example France. Business will be conducted by bankers in France, either British or any other nationality depending simply on who found this area of activity most attractive. This could not be prevented. Banks would, of course, need reserves before they could take deposits and make loans, but these reserves would have to be supplied. If they were not, interest rates would rise in the UK and the purpose of the credit control – restricting credit without raising interest rates – would be entirely frustrated. Accordingly, the controls could be evaded very simply by banks and their customers conducting their sterling business outside the UK.

This was not possible in the past, when exchange controls were around Britain. These controls meant that British residents could not conduct their business outside the UK.

It is, of course, the case that some people will be quicker to find their way around controls than others. Controls would impinge most severely on the unsophisticated. This device, to the extent that it works at all, penalises the poor and the uninformed. That is surely not a desirable outcome.

In conclusion, then, credit controls, if they work, are not painless. But they will not work. They could be evaded simply by going outside the UK. The only kinds of economies which could use credit controls nowadays, even in principle, are economies such as those which Eastern Europe is moving away from – economies where private citizens cannot conduct business whenever they deem it in their own interests, with people outside that country. Moving to such an economy would surely be an extremely high price to pay for being able to use a device, credit controls, which is in any event not a painless way of rationing credit but simply a different way from interest rates.

August 1990

DEVALUATION CAUSES INFLATION

It has become increasingly common in recent months to hear the claim that inflation will rise in this country or that as a result of a currency devaluation. There was concern about that in Britain after sterling fell out of the Exchange Rate Mechanism. Indeed, various forecasters are still disputing how much Britain's inflation will be made worse as a result of that event last September; similar discussion has now started in Spain and in Portugal, following the devaluation of the Peseta and the Escudo. And very generally, the claim that devaluation will cause inflation is used as a major argument against devaluation.

Despite that, the claim is wrong. Devaluation may lead to inflation; but it can never cause inflation.

This is a simple but important distinction that is almost a matter of definition. But although simple and readily understood it is very important in guiding economic policy and in informing discussion of policy.

Inflation is a sustained rise in the general level of prices. A devaluation produces a once-and-for-all reduction in the foreign currency value of a domestic currency. That in turn raises the price of foreign goods relative to domestically produced goods. But just as devaluation produces a one-off decline in the currency's value, so it produces a one-off rise in the price of foreign goods relative to domestic. That need not increase the general level of prices. For it is possible that domestic prices might fall, so that on average prices do not rise. Even if that does not happen, the most that the devaluation can do to the price level of the devaluing country is to raise it once and for all, when the prices of foreign goods rise. It may thus cause an upward step in the price level. That is not an inflation.

It can of course lead to inflation, but that depends on what monetary authorities do, and how wage-rates behave. If the devaluation raises the price level, it makes people worse off. This can lead to claims for higher money wages, to keep their real value – their purchasing power – unchanged. If this happens, the devaluation does not help unemployment fall, for workers are not priced back into jobs. The monetary authorities may be alarmed by unemployment failing to fall. Or, particularly likely, they may be alarmed by unemployment starting to fall, but then rising again as wages go up. They then respond by easing money, and inflation starts to rise.

In other words, a one-off shock to prices can lead to inflation. But it need not. Accordingly, it cannot be said to cause inflation.

Why does such an elementary confusion persist? There are two reasons. One is the perfectly understandable tendency to assume that if one event follows another it is caused by it. The other is that devaluations are quite often the consequence of governments having too expansionary a monetary policy. The consequences of this are concealed until the currency is devalued. And then they appear. Blaming the devaluation – or, quite frequently, the 'speculators' who are asserted to be responsible for it – is then a convenient way for the government to cover up its own mistakes.

But, whatever the reason for its persistence, the idea that devaluation causes inflation is a fallacy. It causes, at most, a once-and-for-all rise in the price level.

June 1993

PRICE RISES ABOVE INFLATION ARE BAD

There is now an annual ritual in London, when fare increases greater than the previous year's inflation are announced for London Transport and British Rail. These increases are denounced for various reasons, *including their being greater than inflation*. The other reasons for objecting to them may be right or wrong; they are not discussed here. The focus of this column is the claim that price increases are bad *because* they are above the rate of inflation.

In one obvious way the objection is just silly. The rate of inflation is an average of price changes. It is almost inevitable that some of these price changes will be above average and some below. (Not quite completely inevitable, because it is possible, though highly unlikely, that every price changes by the same amount; in that case that amount would also be the average price change.) Simply as a matter of arithmetic, then, there is little sense in denouncing price increases because they are above the inflation rate. It is like complaining that some people are above (or below) average height.

There is also another problem, less obvious though at least as important, with objecting to above-inflation – that is, above-average – price rises. Although inflation is measured as an average of price changes, it is fundamentally different from any individual price change. Inflation is a fall in the purchasing power of money, or a rise in the level of prices *in general*. An individual price change is a change in what is called a *relative price* – the price of one good compared to other goods. We measure relative prices in money, but the information they actually convey is how much of one good you have to give up to buy another good (or other goods).

Changes in these relative prices affect both production and consumption. They affect the allocation of resources, by changing incentives to supply goods, and incentives to buy them. Price changes of this sort are useful. In contrast, inflation brings no benefits (although it does help the government to raise revenue).

Hence a price rise above the inflation rate – that is to say, above average – signals that there is a shortage of that good relative to others. The price rise reduces incentives to consume the good and increases incentives to supply it. Price rises below the rate of inflation would send the opposite signals.

Seeing relative prices moving around is in general the symptom of a healthy economy, with innovation going on in production techniques and people's tastes changing in response to increasing prosperity. These price changes can also be bad news, of course, for consumers – an example was the increase in oil prices of some years ago. But even such changes, although unwelcome for some, serve a purpose: they induce consumers to reduce consumption of the good, and to look for substitutes.

It is now possible to draw the above points together. By the nature of the definition of inflation, some price rises must be above inflation and some below. More important, the price changes of individual goods are relative price changes; in contrast, inflation is a fall in the value of money. The former serves a useful purpose, while the latter does not. Indeed, inflation actually impedes the resource-allocating task of relative price changes. For if the average price level is steady – zero inflation – then it is clear that all price changes are relative price changes, to be responded to accordingly. If there is inflation, then it becomes necessary to sort out the extent to which the price change of a good is a price change relative to other goods, and how much is a change in the value of the good relative to money. Only the first part of the price change is a signal to reallocate production and consumption.

If there were no inflation at all, any price rise would be above the rate of inflation. There might well be reasons for complaining about such a price rise, but that it was above the inflation rate would not be one. Complaining on these grounds entails two errors. It shows that there is neither understanding of the definition of inflation, nor understanding of the vital role of relative prices in an economy.

February 1994

RELATIVE PRICE CHANGES CAN BE IGNORED

Recently a charity drew attention to the plight of poor children by arguing that children whose parents were supported by the state were actually worse off than in Victorian times. The claim was that it would cost more than the allowance given for children now to buy the diet which was supplied in Dr Barnardo's homes in the 19th century.

This betrays a misunderstanding of the nature of price indices; these indices are used for two purposes. First, they provide a measure of price changes of goods in general over time – or of the change over time in the value of money. Second, they are used to calculate how 'real' variables – physical quantities – have changed over time. For example, if national income in money terms has doubled, we do not know whether people are better off until we have corrected for any change in prices (that is, 'deflated' it by the price index).

That price index represents the cost of buying a bundle of goods. But it is not a constant bundle of goods. Its physical composition changes over time, for two reasons. Some goods simply disappear from production, or at any rate from widespread use – horse-drawn carriages and candles are examples. They are replaced by other things – in these cases by motor transport and electric light. Others disappear, or have their importance in the index reduced, because of changes in price relative to other goods. If a good becomes more expensive relative to some substitute, consumption of it falls while consumption of the substitute rises.

Not allowing for this by changing the composition of the index would be misleading because the index would no longer reflect what people actually spend their money on, but what they used to spend their money on.

When a good disappears from use because it is obsolete (a horse-drawn carriage) we do not, when calculating a price index, pretend it has not disappeared. Similarly, if a good that had disappeared from consumption because of a price change were kept in the index, we would be measuring the price of a bundle of goods no longer consumed.

Reduced use may appear different – it may seem 'unfair' that people can no longer afford to buy something. But that view neglects the importance of changing relative prices in our economy. They reflect changing relative scarcities. As a good becomes scarce, its price rises, and people are thus induced to look for a substitute. The price system encourages us to economise on scarce resources, and to seek more abundant substitutes, thus maintaining economic efficiency by reducing wastefulness.

Of course, it can seem unfair that the poor may have to pay more heed to those changes than the rich. And it can seem foolish, infuriatingly so on occasions, if a price rise is the result of a misconceived government policy. But to object to the price index on these grounds is to complain about the messenger, not the message.

The price of food is an interesting case. There have been major changes in relative prices not just over the past century, but over much shorter time-periods. Within living memory, chicken has moved from a delicacy to a readily available fairly cheap dish. And over a longer period, oysters have moved from abundance to being a delicacy.

Relative prices change the set of goods which people consume, and this change in turn changes the price index. Compilers of indices thus have a choice. They can either track the price of an underlying bundle of goods, or of a bundle of goods which a 'representative person' buys. The latter has to be interpreted carefully, but it is nevertheless more generally useful than the former. For the former would be substantially influenced by goods consumed in small quantities, or even not consumed at all, because their prices had gone up so much. The information would be accurate but not very interesting. The charity which calculated the price of a particular bundle of goods over a century thus fell into a trap which is often laid by economic data. You can get a precise measure, or a rough-and-ready one. The precise one, however, may give very little information, while the approximation can be very informative when used carefully.

A price index that does not incorporate the effect on behaviour of relative price changes ignores people's response to price signals and thus gives one a piece of almost useless information. Ignoring the effects of relative price changes is always a mistake in economics. The construction of price indices is no exception to that rule. The information that the food consumed by children in Barnardo's in the 19th century would now cost more to buy than an allowance given for the support of children today tells us nothing about children's well-being – because the calculation on which it is based ignores relative price changes.

April 1994

GOVERNMENT-IMPOSED PRICE RISES
HAVE WORSENED INFLATION

Towards the end of 1997 several commentators pointed out that while inflation was still well above the ceiling prescribed by the government, the biggest component of the rise in the retail price index was made up of price rises *imposed* by the government. The following quotation makes the point, and also draws an interesting implication.

> ...much of the inflation now being reported is due to the government's own tax increases. While the headline rate is running at 3.7% and the targeted core increase at 2.8%, the core rate less indirect taxes – VAT, council tax, excise duties, and insurance premium tax – is rising at just 2.1% ... we are in danger of whipping the real economy for inflation visited on it by government policy.

The implication in the above quotation is fallacious because it neglects what would have happened to the general rate of price rises if some particular prices had not gone up: the demand the price increases absorbed would have gone elsewhere, so some other prices would have risen by more than they actually did.

Inflation is determined by monetary policy. But the pattern of *relative* price changes is produced by supply and demand pressures for individual goods. That pattern, some prices rising, some falling, can take place around any average at all – zero or hundreds or thousands of percent per year. That average is determined by one factor, and relative price changes by other, quite different, factors.

The price rises noted in the above quotation were imposed by the government, and were not the result of the voluntary actions of individuals interacting via supply and demand to determine price. But an increase in the relative price of a commodity or group of commodities, however caused, cannot cause inflation.

That is not to say inflation would now be exactly the same as it is had the government-imposed rises not occurred. The relationship between total demand, money growth, and inflation is not tight in the short term at low rates of inflation. Savings behaviour might have been different. People might have been willing to hold more cash and bank deposits. But nevertheless one can be confident of two points. First, if government-dictated prices had not gone up, the price index would not be where it would be if we subtracted their effect from its current level (the 2.1 per cent rate of increase in the quotation). Second, after a period of time the inflation rate would be the same with and without the price rises – what would differ would be the pattern of relative price change around that average.

The second part of the quotation implies that, had it not been for past government action on taxes, monetary policy could have been easier. That implication, although incorrect, leads in a most interesting direction.

Several governments – including the British – have adopted an inflation target. This target can be for different measures of the general price level, or an explicit annual number or range, or just a commitment to 'low' inflation. In no case, though, is there a commitment to zero inflation.

If inflation is bad why not aim to have no inflation at all? One answer is that price indices are biased. By not allowing adequately for quality change or changing patterns of expenditure, as people shift away from goods whose relative prices have risen, they overstate how much the purchasing power of money has fallen. But how much? And is that error constant? In any event, no government has said it is aiming for a non-zero measured rate of inflation because the numbers by which it measures inflation are misleading.

Supposing a government decided it should aim for zero inflation in principle, should it actually do so? There is a possible danger. Because some prices are set, or their change very substantially influenced, by government action, these components of average price change are immune to the pressure of monetary policy, which is therefore greater elsewhere. Allowing relative prices to adjust about a rising average might be the lesser evil given government price pressures.

Of course, tax changes have a one-off effect on prices. So long as governments do not keep on raising taxes the influence of these factors falls away from the price index. It may be appropriate to aim at non-zero inflation while these influences are pushing prices upwards, but if they stop doing so the case for having zero inflation as the inflation target would require serious reconsideration.

To conclude, individual price rises, even those produced by government fiat, do not produce inflation. If monetary policy stayed unchanged then, without these price rises, the pattern of relative price changes would be different, but their average, the rate of inflation, would not be. Although the inflation rate measures the average of changes in relative prices, it is determined by a quite different set of factors from these prices, and cannot be controlled by manipulating them.

March 1998

CONTROLLING PRICES CONTROLS INFLATION

In April this year the *Financial Times* reported that: 'The Spanish Government tried to put the brakes on inflation yesterday by announcing a sweeping package of measures involving cuts in the prices of electricity, gas, and long-distance telephone calls.' The package comprised a set of one-off price cuts in areas of the economy where the Spanish government still has direct influence. This is no more than a variation on an old fallacy – that controlling prices is in itself sufficient to control inflation. Prices in this episode will actually be cut, but on a one-off basis, and then left to be determined by the normal forces of supply and demand.

Inflation is a process of prices rising through time. Just as the price of one good rises when demand exceeds supply, prices in general rise when demand for goods and services in general exceeds supply. Until the excess demand is removed, prices will continue to rise.

Numerous factors can cause prices to rise for a time. For example, a sharp reduction in overall supply can do this. In principle, this should produce a jump in prices, and then its influence is over. But because some prices are slow to change, the process goes on for a time until demand is in line with supply and the price rise comes to a halt. To produce a rise in prices that is not self-limiting, there has to be a continuous pressure keeping demand in excess of supply. This can in principle be produced by a continuous decline in supply – but, at the level of aggregate output rather than in the market for an individual good, this is unknown. (And it is pretty rare in the market for individual goods.)

What can produce this continual excess of aggregate demand? This is easiest to see if one recollects the old – early twentieth century and earlier – definition of inflation. Inflation was then defined as a fall in the purchasing power of money. Such a continual fall could be produced by the supply of money growing year after year faster than the demand for it. This led to attempts to spend the money – on goods, services, and financial and real assets. These attempts bid up prices, and produced a fall in the purchasing power of money. So long as the money supply kept growing too fast, so would prices in general rise and the purchasing power of money fall.

Now let us return to the Spanish 'package'. It is apparent that simply cutting prices will, on the above argument, produce no more than a pause in inflation. Why is the inflation going on? The answer is that Spain is now in the monetary union of Continental Europe, and has no more control over its own monetary policy than, say, Birmingham has over its own monetary policy. Indeed, it no longer makes any sense to talk of Spanish monetary policy. There is a monetary policy for the whole EMU area, of which Spain happens to be a part. And that is Spain's problem. Monetary policy is being set for a (probably somehow weighted) average of the whole of the EMU area, and the interest rate that involves means that demand in Spain is outstripping supply, so prices there are rising. The Spanish government is impotent.

It might, indeed, appear that it has actually made things worse. For by cutting some prices, it has given consumers more spending power. But the matter is actually quite complicated. What the measure has done is increase consumers' spending power but cut that of some other groups which would also have spent. They would probably, of course, have spent on different things, so the pattern of relative price changes will probably be different. But the overall effect will be much the same.

Suppose one does not accept that in the long run money growth causes inflation. Is there any salvation for the Spanish government's measures to be found in rejecting that well-established proposition? Regrettably, even here there is no hope to be found for their measures. Inflation is a *process*, one of continually rising prices. Unless something is done to halt that process prices will continue to rise. One-off cuts will slow this process, but until its cause is removed, the process will continue.

What will halt Spanish inflation? Rising prices in Spain will make production expensive there relative to the rest of the EU, and will also direct non-Spanish demand away from Spanish goods. Factories will close or move away. The excess demand will abate, and the inflation slow. These pressures will bear particularly hard on goods that can be readily traded and on production processes that can readily move; but they will eventually slow the rise in Spanish prices.

To conclude, the Spanish policy of cutting prices to control inflation is just a new version of controlling prices so as to control inflation. Until what is causing the inflation is removed, the inflation continues. Likewise, it will continue in Spain when prices are cut. Now that Spain no longer has control of its own monetary policy, the Spanish government has no control over Spanish inflation.

September 1999

INFLATION, REAL VALUES AND 'GOVERNMENT MONEY'

On 1 September 1999, a headline as follows appeared in a British national newspaper: 'Inflation fall puts Treasury in dilemma.' What had happened, and what was the problem thought to be?

On the previous day, the latest UK inflation data had been published, showing that Britain's retail price index (RPI) had risen by 1.1 per cent over the preceding 12 months. That was the lowest 12-month rise for over 30 years – surely unqualified good news in a country with a record of high and fluctuating inflation. Not only had inflation fallen, but unemployment too fell, according to unemployment data published a few days subsequently. How did the commentators find a problem in that?

They wrote, 'But the bigger than forecast drop in inflation presents a dilemma for Gordon Brown, the Chancellor. It means he faces the prospect of giving single pensioners a rise of less than £1 a week next April – the lowest for years – at a time when the economy is growing and tax revenues buoyant.'

By writing thus, they committed no fewer than three fallacies. How?

The Chancellor's commitment is to increase the *money* value of pensions every year in line with the rise in the price level, so as to keep the *real* value of pensions (and some other payments) unchanged.

Now, the inflation rate over the previous 12 months shows the rise in the price level over that period. Hence the first error in the newspaper story. It was not the 'drop' in inflation that meant the Chancellor is obliged to increase pensions by a small money amount, but the *level* of inflation. (That the 'drop' was 'bigger than forecast' is of course completely irrelevant to the discussion.)

Now to the next error. The Chancellor's commitment is to maintain the *real* value – the purchasing power – of the pensions and other payments which are linked to the RPI. That the writers of the article are fundamentally confused over the difference between real and money values is shown by the sentence they used to illustrate how much of a money increase a single pensioner would receive under indexation.

> This [i.e. indexation] would mean a single person's basic state pension going up by only 75 pence a week – enough to buy a packet of peanuts – to £66.75.

The increase, of course, would allow the pensioner to keep on buying what he or she bought at the start of the previous year: for the increase would be compensation for the rise in prices over that period. The purpose of indexation is not to produce an *increase* in purchasing power – not even to the extent of a packet of peanuts – but to keep purchasing power unchanged. Hence, whether he or she has to hand over a large or a small amount of money does not matter from the point of view of the commitment. So long as the real value is maintained, so is the commitment honoured. That was the second error.

Now to the third. Look again at the quotation. The Chancellor, they wrote, '...faces the prospect of giving single pensioners less than £1 a week...'

The Chancellor may well be personally a very generous man. Despite their public image, many Scots are generous supporters of deserving causes, albeit in an unostentatious and private way. But however generous the Chancellor may be, he could not conceivably give even 50 pence to every pensioner and other recipient of index-linked benefits in the country. His income would not allow it. What the writers meant is that the Chancellor would be transferring money from one group of people to another, through the tax system. The government has no income except what it either takes through taxation or borrows.

The point is an important one, for the idea that there is something called 'government money' muddles many discussions. There are calls for more public spending because the government is in budget surplus, with tax revenues exceeding spending. Why should that automatically mean more must be spent? More government spending would mean less of some other kind of spending. The government has no sack of gold from which it can make disbursements, spreading wealth all around. It only has what it has first taken away.

So, three errors were concentrated into a few lines in the article. First, there was confusion between a fall in inflation and low inflation. Second, there was failure to understand that if inflation is low, prices in money terms do not go up much every year. Third, and most important because it demonstrated a widespread fallacy, was the notion that the government has resources it can give away. It has resources only if it takes them first. Every spending programme must thus be evaluated against competing alternatives, which always include spending by the private sector. The fallacy that the government has resources to give away is particularly dangerous.

March 2000

CONFUSION ABOUT INFLATION

Inflation is just the sum of changes in the price index:
reduce any one and inflation will fall.

For some three years now the Bank of England has had a
target for inflation. It has been told to aim within a range
of 1.5 per cent per annum to 3.5 per cent for inflation as
measured by RPI-X: that is to say, by the retail price index
change excluding any change in mortgage interest rates.
Inflation has consistently been in the lower half of that
range. At the end of last year, some commentators started
to say that, because of that fact, and one other, the Bank
could safely cut the interest rate which it sets to control
monetary conditions. The other fact was that the price
of oil had risen sharply, and that, it was asserted, was
some sort of special factor. Had that not happened, it was
claimed, inflation would have been lower.

There are actually two confusions behind that recommendation. The first is confusion about the facts, and
the second a fundamental confusion about the nature of
inflation.

First, the facts. The price of oil had risen in Britain for
two reasons. Demand for oil on world markets had pulled

up the oil price in terms of the currency in which that price is quoted – the US dollar. Second, sterling, far from being 'strong' (as some advocates of devaluation had claimed), had in fact weakened against the US dollar. (Sterling had also been weak against the yen. It had been strong only against the crumbling euro.) It seems highly likely that interest rate cuts would have weakened sterling still further against the dollar, hence in time driving up still further the sterling price of oil. So, on these simple factual grounds alone, it is false to assert that the sterling price of oil (the price that matters for UK inflation) is independent of the Bank of England's monetary policy.

That, then, is the factual confusion, Now to the second confusion behind the argument, the fallacious definition of inflation.

As a matter of arithmetic it is of course true that inflation is the sum of the price changes of all the goods which make up the retail price index. *But these price changes are not independent one of another.*

Oil gives us a good example – so let us pursue the argument using as an illustration a change in the oil price. Once the example has been set out, the argument can then be generalised.

The oil price rose in sterling terms in 1999. Suppose it had not, and that nothing else apart from that supposition changed in that year's situation. The lower oil price would have meant that people in Britain could either spend more on other things, or buy more oil, or of course both. Spending what they did not spend on oil on other goods would have pushed up the prices of other goods – so while the oil price had not gone up, other prices in the price index would have gone up instead. The price index as a whole would still have risen. What if (as it happens, given what we know of spending habits, an unlikely case) more oil had been bought, then what would have happened? The price index reflects both the prices of goods bought, and the share of those goods in individuals' expenditures. If they increase the share spent on oil, then the share of oil in the index goes up, and therefore with an unchanged oil price the index goes up.

That, it should be made clear, is the principle of the matter. In practice the composition of the price index changes with a lag. So if the oil price had stayed the same rather than risen, and the money that was spent on oil as a result of the higher oil price was instead spent entirely in buying more oil at the unchanged price, inflation as measured would not have gone up so much. But that would represent not slower inflation, but an error in the measurement of inflation until the shares of different goods in the RPI were changed to reflect the new spending patterns.

Again, then, there is no fall in inflation. And of course the same conclusion holds if, in consequence of the low oil price, more was spent on other goods and also on oil. Again inflation would be more or less unchanged. The claim that if one price had been lower inflation would have been lower is plainly false, and the recommendation for a change in interest rates based on it is, equally plainly, foolish.

Fundamentally, the confusion is over the nature of inflation. Inflation is a fall, year after year, in the purchasing power of money. It results from the supply of money growing faster than the demand for it. The Bank of England adjusts interest rates so as to prevent the value of money falling faster than (on average) 2.5 per cent per annum. Temporary fluctuations in the rate of inflation can have a variety of causes. But only the Bank of England's monetary policy can have a durable effect on the long-term rate of inflation. The idea that that rate is affected by a change in the price of any one good reflects profoundly muddled thinking about the nature of inflation. Inflation is a monetary phenomenon, not the sum of independent price changes.

March 2001

PART 4

FISCAL POLICY: TAXATION

GOVERNMENTS CAN PRECISELY MANAGE
THE ECONOMY BY FISCAL POLICY

With the latest budget we again heard cries that the Chancellor should 'take some more out of the economy', that taxes should go higher, usually to raise some precisely specified amount of revenue, and so have a precisely specified effect on aggregate demand. Had the economy been in recession, we would no doubt have heard exactly the opposite recommendations, couched in exactly the same language.

The idea is nonsense. The government's tax and spending policies do affect the economy. But their effect on demand is primarily in its composition. To the extent that they affect the level of demand, the effect is uncertain both in size and duration.

To see this, consider the current situation. The government was running a surplus, its revenue exceeded its expenditure. This meant it was repaying debt. The instruction to 'take more out of the economy' meant repay more debt. In other words, someone would pay more taxes to the government so that the government would redeem debt held by someone else. Person A's disposable income would have been reduced so that person B's capital could be converted from bonds to a bank deposit.

Now, how is that supposed to affect demand? The effect on A's spending is not precisely known. If he expects taxes to be lower in the future – as a result of lower debt service costs – he will not cut back his spending by the full amount of his tax increase.

And what of person B? What happens to his savings? They will be spent. Or they will be lent to somebody else, who assuredly does not borrow them with the intention of not spending them. If they are left in a bank deposit, they will be lent to a spender – by the bank.

There will of course be delays. Person B may take some time to think what to do. His borrower may take some time to spend. During such delays, spending will dip. But only during the adjustment period. And how long this will be, no one can say.

In summary, fiscal policy relies on lags in adjustment. These are lags whose length we can neither explain nor predict. Fine tuning by fiscal policy is impossible.

Recommending it presumes more knowledge about the economy than we have now and are ever likely to have.

June 1990

EMPLOYERS CONTRIBUTE TOWARDS
WORKERS' BENEFITS

A Labour Party spokesman recently declared that, whatever changes the Labour Party was considering in the scope or rates of National Insurance contributions, an employer's contribution would be retained. The reason given for this was that by levying that contribution, it was ensured that employers contributed towards health and retirement benefits for those they employed.

This is an example of a very old and very common economic fallacy. Believing it is certainly not confined to Labour Party spokesmen. Examples could be found in any country, and from every political party. The example noted above is simply a recent one.

The fallacy is to believe that the government has any ability whatsoever to control who bears the burden of a tax.

To avoid confusion it should be said explicitly that for the purposes of this analysis National Insurance is like a tax, in that it is a compulsory levy charged by government – on income in this case. It differs from other taxes in that it is purportedly allocated to the provision of certain specified benefits, but that distinction is not relevant for this present purpose. What matters here is that it is, like income tax, a compulsory charge on income. It does, however, differ from income tax in that part of it is 'paid' by the employer. That might seem to settle the question. The employer is obliged to pay it by law; so that is their contribution. But that is not the case.

National Insurance contributions, be they employers' or employees', like income tax, create a gap between what the employer pays and what the employee receives. In the absence of all taxes and other compulsory charges on income, the employer's average costs per worker and a worker's earnings would be the same. But compulsory payments change that situation. Suppose the law is that of every £100 the worker earns, he can keep £90, and £10 goes to the government. The law could say that he first gets his £100 and has to hand over £10 – the employee has the legal liability to pay; or it could say that the £10 is deducted by the employer before each £100 is handed over – the employer has the legal liability to pay. Now, what does the assignment of legal liability affect? It affects neither the fact that if the employee wants to keep £100, he has to earn more than that; nor the fact that if the employer wants £100 worth of work supplied, he has to pay more than £100.

So the first, and fundamental, point is that the charge increases the cost of obtaining labour; and also means that to earn £100, more than £100 worth of labour has to be supplied. Seeing that leads on to discussion of who bears the cost, and why.

Think for simplicity of a situation with one worker and one employer. The worker can vary the hours he works, and the employer can choose to buy a variable amount of hours. Other things equal, we would expect the worker to be willing to work more hours the more he was paid per hour. Similarly, the less each hour of work cost, the more of them would the employer buy.

The worker and his employer would negotiate, and discover that at some wage rate the amount of hours the worker was willing to work equalled the amount the employer wanted to buy at that wage rate. That would be the wage rate agreed, and the hours worked would be what the employer and employee both wanted at that rate of pay per hour. That can be called the 'pre-tax equilibrium' situation. Now suppose a tax is imposed. Continuing with the above numbers, suppose the tax is at a 10 per cent flat rate; for any £100 earned, £10 tax is paid. Initially (if a contract of any reasonable duration exists between employer and employee) nothing changes. The employee works the same number of hours as before, receives the same payment as before, and 10 per cent of that payment is handed over.

Notice that even at this stage, before renegotiation, where the legal burden to pay the tax lies is immaterial. The employer pays a certain amount, and the employee keeps 90 per cent of that amount. This is true whether the wage is paid over before or after the tax is deducted. But that situation is not an equilibrium. Nothing has changed for the employer; but the employee is getting less pay per hour than before. If content before, he certainly is not content now. As soon as allowed under the contract, renegotiation will take place. The employee will wish to work somewhat fewer hours, at a higher rate per hour (since he keeps less of what he earns); and since more is being demanded per hour, the employer will wish to buy fewer hours. Eventually, a new situation, the 'post-tax equilibrium', will be reached. Fewer hours of work will be supplied, and a higher wage rate per hour will be paid.

There will be a change in the amount earned before tax, and 10 per cent of this changed amount will be handed over as tax. None of this is affected by where the legal burden to pay the tax is placed. What has happened is that a gap has been created between what the employer pays and what the employee receives; wage costs now exceed earnings. This leads the employer to cut back demand, and the employee to cut back supply. By how much is each cut back? This depends on how sensitive each is to changes in price. The more sensitive, the greater will be the change in supply or in demand.

The 'cost' of the tax is thus shared between employer and employee. The employee earns less per hour and works fewer hours; the employer pays more per hour, but employs the worker for fewer hours. The distribution of these changes depends solely on the respective sensitivity to wage changes of employer's demand and employee's supply, and on nothing else. Where the legal obligation lies is immaterial.

The above description can of course be extended to a situation with many employers and many employees. Here hours worked might vary; and numbers employed would almost certainly also change. But the crucial characteristics of the post-tax equilibrium would be unchanged. Every hour of work would cost employers more than workers received for it. The gap would be tax.

The introduction of the tax would reduce demand for workers, and reduce willingness to work. How the burden was shared would depend on no legal obligation; but on sensitivity of demand and supply to changes in wage rates.

Claiming the fact that the law saying a particular person or group pays a tax determines who pays it, is a fallacy. The location of the legal obligation to hand over the money to the government is immaterial in determining who bears the tax. Government can no more legislate for that than it can legislate for the sun always to shine at Wimbledon.

September 1996

TAXES SHOULD GO UP TO SLOW INFLATION

In the spring and early summer of 1997, almost every commentator on the British economy (with the notable exception of Samuel Brittan) argued that inflation in Britain was starting to accelerate, and that taxes should be raised (or public spending cut) to stop it. Now, it may or may not be the case that inflation was accelerating; and there may or may not have been a case for raising taxes or cutting spending so as to reduce government borrowing. Neither of these points is considered here. The focus is on the claim that a rise in taxes will slow inflation. That claim is a fallacy, but a somewhat complex one, in that there is one set of extraordinary circumstances where it is justified. Those circumstances are discussed briefly below. But in general, and certainly in Britain today, a rise in taxes does not stop inflation. That point can be made first by analysis and then reinforced by evidence.

A useful starting point is a definition of inflation. Inflation is a long-lasting rise in the general level of prices. It is a rise which goes on until something changes to stop it. This is in contrast to a change in the price level, which is a move from one price level to another, at which the price level then stays.

The fact that inflation is a continuous process should immediately make one pause before claiming that a rise in taxes will stop it. Unless the price level is like an imaginary frictionless ball on an imaginary frictionless (and infinitely large) billiard table – in which case one tap would set it moving forever – for inflation one should look for a cause that is present so long as the inflation is present. One should look for a *continuous cause for a continuous process.*

It might be claimed that a tax increase *would* remove a continuous cause, for the cause is 'excess demand' – demand greater than can be supplied without upward price pressure. Can a tax increase do that? What is to be done with the tax revenue? If it is not to be spent by its recipient, the government, then it will reduce government borrowing, lead to debt repayment, or, in the extraordinary case where a government not only is not borrowing but has no debts to repay, to the government acquiring assets.

Consider the expenditure consequences of each of these in turn. If less is borrowed, then the money which was to be lent will be lent or spent elsewhere. It will not just vanish. If the taxes are used to repay existing debts, then the recipient of the repayment will in turn do something with it – lend (to someone who will spend) – or spend directly. (Of course no one would claim that the pattern of spending will not be affected, but that is a different matter.) And exactly the same applies to the acquisition of assets. If these are acquired from the domestic private sector, the recipients have money to spend.

It might be objected at this point that the above arguments seem to deny the existence, even in principle, of the

Keynesian 'multiplier'. That, it may be recollected, claimed to show that (for example) a rise in government spending financed by a rise in taxes would lead to an increase in total spending, as private expenditure would fall by less than the rise in taxes. How can that be?

People must somehow cut their expenditure by less than the rise in taxes – which they can only do by saving less. What happens to the people who were borrowing those savings? They will be unable to spend. This does not end up reducing private spending by as much as government spending goes up only if that private saving was somehow sitting there unused – a possibility perhaps in a depression, with the price level actually falling so that people defer spending in the expectation that 'prices will be lower tomorrow'. But we are not dealing with that, but with the problem of *inflation*; so that special case need not be considered further.

So far, then, it has been argued that there are two problems with the claim that a rise in taxes will slow inflation. First, inflation is a continuous process but a rise in taxes is a one-off cause, so it is hard to argue that the latter will stop the former. Second, the effects of a rise in taxes on private sector spending have been considered, and it has been shown that certainly in an environment of strong demand and rising prices, a rise in taxes cannot be expected to reduce total spending, by the government and the private sector combined (although it may well change its composition).

So much for analysis. What about evidence? The evidence goes the same way. The effects of tax increases on spending are uncertain – uncertain both in size and in timing. Evidence can be drawn both from the UK and overseas. First, the UK. In 1967 fiscal policy was tightened after a devaluation. There was no balance-of-payments effect. That only came when domestic demand was squeezed by a monetary tightening. Looking further back in history, we find inflation rising and falling with no associated changes in taxes: for example, prices fell on average from 1870 to the early 1890s, and then rose steadily to 1914. But there was no matching change (or even series of changes) in taxes. And in the USA, in the late 1960s, a tax increase was imposed but inflation continued until monetary policy was tightened.

In short, the evidence does not suggest that in general a fiscal tightening is necessary or sufficient to slow inflation. What of the special case mentioned earlier? This is when governments are financing their expenditure by money creation rather than by taxing or borrowing. Almost every hyperinflation – an inflation greater than 50 per cent per month – has resulted from such behaviour. Tax increases to stop money creation would then be necessary to stop the hyperinflation. But governments generally got into that situation because they had lost the political support to let them raise taxes – so the recommendation is desirable but not possible.

In normal times a tax increase (or a spending cut) might, via reducing government borrowing, reduce interest rates, and this might induce people to hold more money, thus reducing the excess of money supply over money demand. But this would be a once only effect on the excess *stock* of money; to slow inflation a fall in the *rate of growth* of excess money is necessary.

To conclude, the claim that a rise in taxes will slow inflation is without analytical foundation (except in the case of hyperinflation) and is inconsistent with the facts. There is therefore absolutely no reason why taxes in Britain should go up to slow inflation.

September 1997

THE GOVERNMENT SHOULD PLACE EXTRA TAXES ON COMPANIES THAT MAKE 'EXCESS PROFITS'

For many centuries, from when governments first gathered taxes, the only criterion when designing a tax was how easy it was to collect. Ease of collection still matters. But recently another factor has started to be considered. Does the tax influence behaviour? Taxes on tobacco, for example, are high in Britain on the grounds that consumption of it should be discouraged. (It is of course entirely by chance that the tax brings in substantial revenue.) Much harder to find are taxes which do not affect behaviour, which are in general the sort one wants because they avoid 'distorting' people's behaviour. People usually know best for themselves what they want to do and what they want to consume so as to achieve the highest level of well-being they can. Taxes which interfere with this are undesirable – but it is hard to design ones which do not.

In this regard, the classic poll tax is ideal. A tax paid by everyone, where everyone pays the same, and pays it until, for example, death, might perhaps induce suicide among those who object on principle to paying taxes, but would not in general affect behaviour once the decision that paying the tax was preferable to being dead had been taken.

Running a close second is a 'windfall' tax – a tax levied on the benefit someone has received purely by chance. Since the gain is pure chance, and came with no premeditation, prior planning or prior action taken with the aim of receiving the gain, a tax on the windfall could not affect future behaviour. The principle is clear. But in practice matters are not so easy. Pure windfalls are hard to find. A lottery win is not a windfall – a ticket has to be bought.

One can imagine windfall profits taxes; but they too are hard to find. An example might be where a firm sets out to discover iron ore, and discovers, quite by chance, a gold mine. And what about taxes on excess, or windfall, profits in general? There are two fundamental problems with them – identification and time consistency. They are discussed in turn.

When is a profit a windfall or an excess? The case of the iron-seeker who found gold – where one activity by pure chance generates entirely unpredictably high returns – is rather rare. Profits simply higher than other firms' will not do. They could represent effort or skill – indeed, if they persist for years, they must reflect either that or monopoly. (If they are the result of monopoly the appropriate response is not to tax them but to eliminate the monopoly – otherwise an inefficiency is being allowed simply so the government can raise revenue.)

If the high profit is the result of effort or skill, it is not a windfall – even if the skill were the result of chance inheritance, it is likely that it had to be practised and certain that it had to be applied to bring in profits. So the simple method of examining profits and comparing them with profits earned elsewhere cannot reveal excesses.

What about comparing them with expectations? Here there is a different range of problems. Expectations might have been too low. That was plainly the case with the previously nationalised utilities in the UK. Few – possibly not even their managers – were aware of the degree of inefficiency that public-sector ownership had produced, so few expected the efficiency gains or foresaw the level of profits.

The problems of measuring 'excess profits', of even knowing when one sees them, arise from the woolliness of the concept. The term is easy to use, but not to define.

What about avoiding the problem, and simply declaring that, say, for a particular *past* year taxes will be higher than previously announced? That may appear to avoid distortions – after all, we cannot change our past behaviour. Nevertheless, such taxes also distort decisions – for even if the government promises never to do it again, who would believe it? There is no way a government could bind itself to behave through time consistently with its promises – no way to guarantee that it is 'time consistent'.

The notion that 'windfall' or 'excess' profits taxes (or taxes on anything else) can avoid distorting behaviour is a delusion. It may well be a delusion fostered deliberately, of course, in an attempt to fool people into imagining they will not be affected by taxes. But delusion it is. The idea that taxes can be gathered without affecting economic efficiency is almost without exception false. The claim that 'excess profits' can be readily identified, and then taxed without affecting efficiency, is an example either of error or dishonesty.

December 1997

THE CHANCELLOR CAN PREDICT THE EFFECT
OF TAX ALLOWANCES ON BEHAVIOUR

As this column is being written (in late February 2001), Spring is coming on, and so is the Chancellor's 2001 Budget. Spring brings its crop of fresh-sprouting flowers, and the Budget brings its crop of fresh-sprouting economic fallacies. Not all of these are from the Chancellor, of course; Budget commentators supply a good few. And, it should be emphasised, the present Chancellor is far from the only one to give us a bouquet of fallacies from which we can choose and then dissect a sample. Previous Chancellors from both parties which have held office have also been generous with their gifts.

What is particularly striking about the present Chancellor, though, is his proclivity to reward Virtue and punish Vice. (It has to be remarked how that can sometimes lead him to do strange things. He does, for example, reward working families by tax credits; but then penalises them if either of the parents drives to work to support the family. But be that as it may, it is on the general policy and not on its particular perversities that this discussion focuses.)

The general fallacy in question is closely related to one that has been exposed in previous chapters. A few words on that will help set the scene.

What might be called the 'foundation fallacy' is that the Chancellor can decide who pays a tax. He can impose a tax on a good – petrol, for example; but the effect this will have on the price the purchaser pays, and on what the supplier receives, depends on how responsive supply and demand are to price changes. The Chancellor by his tax creates a gap between what the buyer pays and what the supplier receives. He cannot fix the extent to which it leads to a rise in price to the user and how much it leads to a fall in price to the producer. If, for example, consumers' demand is totally insensitive to price, then consumers will not change how much they demand, suppliers will not change how much they supply, and the price will go up by the amount of the tax.

Now to the present fallacy, holding in our minds the crucial importance of the price sensitivity of demand and supply in determining how prices and quantities of a good respond to the imposition of a tax (or of course the granting of a subsidy) on the good.

Subsidising the good will, just as tax does, create a gap between what the buyer pays and what the supplier receives. But this time, rather than raising the price to buyers and lowering what is received to producers, the opposite happens. Producers receive more, and buyers have to hand over less. Just as in the case of the tax, though, how much of the subsidy goes as higher prices to the producer and how much as lower prices to the consumer depends on how responsive supply and demand are to changes in price.

Now, in the course of his attempts to punish Vice and reward Virtue, the Chancellor is interested in the effects on *quantities*, not in those on prices. But the two are inextricably interrelated. He cannot know the effect on price because he does not know how sensitive supply and demand are to price changes. And, for exactly the same reason, he cannot know the effect his measures will have in encouraging some activities and discouraging others. Take as an example some activity where the amount of it people are willing to do is independent of price. (It is hard to imagine one totally insensitive to price, but doing so makes for a simple example.) Subsidising it will simply lower the price a buyer of that activity has to pay, but no more will be consumed – because no more is being supplied for consumption.

Hence, unless the Chancellor knows the supply-and-demand sensitivities for any activity he seeks to either encourage or discourage, he has no idea whatsoever of the effectiveness of his measures.

Further, there is yet another problem. The Chancellor commits so much revenue, or imposes so much tax, on each unit of the activity. He has to calculate the cost of subsidies and taxes before he knows what his actions will do to government borrowing (or debt repayment). But since he does not know how much the activities subsidised or taxed will change as a result of his taxes and subsidies, he does not know the cost of his policies. In short, not only are the effects of trying to encourage Virtue and discourage

Vice unpredictable; the very trying to do so makes projections of budget surpluses or deficits even less reliable than before. And all this follows because it is fallacious to believe that the Chancellor can predict the effect of tax allowances on behaviour.

June 2001

PART 5

FISCAL POLICY: GOVERNMENT SPENDING

BRITAIN IS NOT INVESTING ENOUGH

Exhortations to invest more are common. Opposition parties (in every country) are habitually accusing governments of 'under-investing' in this or that. Sometimes the criticism is truly fatuous, and governments are urged to 'invest more in our future' – as if we could invest in the past, perhaps in last year or the last century. But even when that particular stupidity is not perpetrated, the advice to invest more is not necessarily sound.

People can spend their incomes on the consumption of goods and services, or they can save. Before there can be investment there has to be saving. Investment, in other words, is *deferred consumption.*

It may have been deferred so that more can be consumed later. It may have been deferred simply to enable there to be consumption later – an important reason for saving by individuals with volatile incomes. Or it may have been deferred so that it can augment the consumption of future generations by being bequeathed to descendants.

But whatever the motive (except in the rare case of the individual who accumulates savings simply for the pleasure of accumulation and with no other end in view), saving, and hence investment, is not an end in itself. It is a means of achieving an end. Therefore in turn it is only desirable to increase investment if doing so furthers the achievement of that end, and does so at a price worth paying.

In other words, the return on the investment is of great importance. When politicians urge more investment, they should think both about what the return on it will be, and what is being given up by that investment. Does the benefit of the return exceed the benefit that would have come from what has to be given up? That is the crucial question, and despite being crucial it is often ignored.

We frequently hear it claimed that Britain is investing too little in this or that compared to 'overseas competition'. (The notion that countries rather than firms compete with one another is also a fallacy, and has been dealt with on pages 32–35.) But looking at the amount invested in different countries, and saying we should increase ours to that of the highest, is simply wrong. For the costs of investing elsewhere may be lower, or the returns higher, or both. It can be worth investigating, and is always worth thinking about, why investment (relative to, say, income) differs in different countries. But the simple fact of difference in itself can justify only that investigation. It cannot justify trying to increase investment forthwith.

This is the more so because, starting from the notion that investment is a desirable end in itself, calling something investment is then thought to justify expenditure on it with no more ado. The concept of investment in education is an interesting example. We are told to 'invest more in education'. What does this mean? It has been applied, for example, to increasing the salaries of school teachers. Now, there may or may not be a case for that. But increasing the wages of providers of services is about as far away from investment – that is to say, the purchase of a durable asset which provides a stream of service in the future – as we can get!

There are also claims, derived from some modern theories of the causes of economic growth, that investment will raise an economy's growth rate. By this is meant not just that it can temporarily boost demand, but that it can produce a sustainable rise in the rate of increase per head. If achievable, that is certainly desirable. This modern growth theory can support such claims; but in a very precise way, not the broad-brush way in which it has been seized on by advocates of increased state intervention in the economy. The theory essentially says that certain types of investment may need to be encouraged to raise an economy's growth rate because they provide generalised benefits – benefits which do not accrue only to the investor. The theory does not say that raising any type of investment by subsidy from the general body of taxpayers will raise the growth rate.

To conclude, the basic fallacy behind the claim that we should invest more is to confuse outputs and inputs, ends and means. Investment is the deferral of the ultimate aim of economic activity, consumption. It is therefore a cost.

No-one has yet claimed – to my knowledge anyway – that if one uses lots of labour as compared with another firm or country to produce some good then that is desirable. Exactly the same applies to investment. Investment is a cost of production. We should invest as efficiently as possible, not as much as possible.

December 1996

GOVERNMENT BORROWING SHOULD BE GUIDED BY THE 'GOLDEN RULE'

'Government borrowing should be guided by the "Golden Rule". Over the course of a business cycle, government should borrow only for investment.' Or so, at least, the present Chancellor of the Exchequer tells us. But his advice is fallacious, and his describing it as the 'Golden Rule' is puzzling.

What rule should govern government borrowing? The basic principle relates to the overall *total* of debt which should not grow faster than national income. If it does, the costs of debt service (interest) will rise and taxes will have to go up to pay the interest.

When taxes and debt are low, taxpayers may well not be fully aware of the future tax consequences of current borrowing, so government spending can for a time rise unhindered by taxpayers' objections. But as debt goes higher relative to income, interest rates start to rise for fear the debt will not be repaid; the costs of servicing the debt become still greater; and the government may resort to printing money. Inflation then takes off – in the extreme to hyperinflation (more than 50 per cent per month).

Almost all great inflations have resulted from debt growing out of control. Accordingly, the principle that debt should not grow faster than income is well founded in both theory and evidence.

The Chancellor did, however, lay down a rather different rule: that government should over the business cycle borrow only to the extent that it is investing. That rule prompts three questions. Why should government borrow at all? What is investment? And why should government borrow to pay for it?

For good reasons, individuals, when their income varies, do not immediately vary their expenditure in line. Change itself is costly. In addition, a general rule is that, as you have more of something, the pleasure obtained from a little more decreases. Likewise, the less you have of something the more you miss a little less. Individuals therefore dampen consumption changes.

It makes good sense for governments to do the same. Not because they would themselves experience losses if they did otherwise (except perhaps of votes) but the recipients of their expenditure would. Alternatively, if governments kept their spending steady, and varied tax rates so that tax revenue stayed steady in the face of income fluctuations, the changes in tax rates would be disruptive to firms and individuals. In summary, it is as sensible for governments to borrow and then repay to smooth out their income fluctuations as it is for individuals. This corresponds roughly to 'no borrowing over the business cycle' only so long as the upswings and downswings are regular and equal, which they may well not be – so in this regard

Gordon Brown's 'principle' is just a first approximation to prudent behaviour rather than a fundamental rule of sound finance.

What is investment? In the private sector it is the outlay of a sum of money now so that it can yield a stream of income for some time ahead. But most government investment is not intended to yield a cash return. Any return may not be in the form of cash, or only to some extent in that form – the return may, for example, be spread so widely that charging is impracticable. It is easy to justify 'investments' whose out-turn cannot readily be measured.

There is a classic 'pay as you use' principle of public finance. Projects which yield future benefits should be financed by borrowing. The argument is that borrowing raises interest rates and reduces private investment now, so that future benefits are not all at the expense of the current generation's consumption. But although correct in principle, and operational when public investment involved such matters as building bridges or fighting a war against a foreign enemy, it would be easy nowadays to justify all sorts of borrowing by this argument.

That leads to the last question. Why borrow for investment? The classic reason is because doing so crowds out private investment. That is desirable on the above argument so long as we are sure that government investment is at least as productive as private investment.

To summarise, there is nothing special or long-established about the Chancellor's 'rule'. Governments *should* borrow so that fluctuations in income produce fluctuations neither in spending nor in taxes. That *may* lead to no net borrowing over the business cycle, but it *need* not. Public investment *should* be financed by borrowing, to ensure that future recipients of benefits pay for them. But again, following that rule is no guarantee of prudence. The rule is easily fudged, especially in an era when politicians talk of 'investing for the future' (can we invest for the past?), or describe raising salaries of teachers (possibly desirable, but on other grounds) as 'investing in education'.

And what of calling this vague guide to sensible policy the 'Golden Rule'? It has never been called that before. It certainly does not guarantee good outcomes, nor does it have the solid intellectual underpinnings, or even the justification by experience, that the name suggests.

June 1998

WELFARE BENEFITS SHOULD NOT BE CUT WHEN THE PUBLIC FINANCES ARE IN SURPLUS

'...it seems curious the government is cutting future benefits for lone parents ... just as the public finances are heading towards surplus.' (*Financial Times*, 20 November 1997)

The above quotation embodies what one hopes is a fallacy – that government is shorter-sighted in its planning than are the private citizens of the country which elected it.

When that quotation appeared, the British economy was booming, growing a good way above its likely sustainable long-term average. This has considerable significance for the government's finances. Both its revenue and its expenditure are affected.

The government budget is said to be in surplus when revenue from taxation exceeds all forms of expenditure, and in deficit when expenditure exceeds tax revenue. When the economy booms, tax revenue automatically rises because people are earning more and spending more, so pay more in all forms of taxation. At the same time, government expenditure grows more slowly. (Expenditure can fall, but in Britain since 1950 a fall is an extraordinarily rare event.) This slower growth is produced by 'cyclical' factors such as unemployment benefit falling off as more people move into the workforce.

Hence, in a boom, tax revenue catches up on spending, and can exceed it. This is the basis of the comment in the opening quotation. If tax revenue is catching up on spending, perhaps passing it, why cut benefits paid to a particular group of poor people?

There are numerous 'microeconomic' answers that focus on the nature of the benefit, arguing that it promotes behaviour which is in the long run damaging to the individuals concerned, for example.

But there is also a 'macroeconomic' answer – to see it, it is useful to consider what would happen if spending were allowed to rise because tax revenue was going up. In the past the government has borrowed to pay for some of its spending. This borrowing has to be paid back. At least, the lenders expect it will be; and if it is not, they will be reluctant to lend in the future. How can the borrowing be paid back?

One route of course is by further borrowing, in effect just rolling over the debt. That would be a perfectly sustainable policy if there were never any new borrowing, and the stock of debt never grew. But if new debt were issued, then the stock of debt would be growing all the time, the costs of debt service would rise, interest rates on the debt would rise as lenders started to fear they might not be repaid, and taxes would take an increasing share of national income just to service the debt. If this is to be prevented debt must be repaid; or, at the very least, held to a growth rate lower than national income.

How can that be done? When the economy slows, government revenue slows while expenditure rises; so debt goes up. Hence, when the economy is booming, advantage must be taken of the opposite effect. Strong tax revenues and slower government spending must be used not to encourage new spending but to slow the growth of debt, and even to repay it.

It is no mere theoretical possibility that problems will arise if governments behave otherwise. Almost every great inflation in history has followed from loss of control of government spending. As debt increased, fresh debt became harder to sell; and resistance to taxes increased as the burden of taxation rose. Governments then turned to their third source of finance – they printed money to pay their bills. Inflation soared, and the economies without exception collapsed soon after, often in civil war or revolution.

That may seem a long way from cuts in lone-parent benefit. And indeed it is. But they are only one item among a vast number of government spending programmes. Each one of these should be justified, not just allowed to continue because tax revenue is buoyant. Otherwise the government would be more short-sighted than voters, spending today because it has the money, regardless of what income and what expenditure obligations it will have tomorrow. Few individuals behave that way; and of the few who do, most do it because they are poor, not because they are short-sighted about future obligations. And of course, individuals are entitled to be short-sighted if they wish; the main consequences of such behaviour fall on themselves. But if government acts in a short-sighted fashion, allowing its debt to grow year after year, the consequences fall not just on the individual members of the culpable government, but on all the citizens of the country, who are damaged by their government being less prudent then they are.

There may – or may not – be arguments for continuing with the payment of single-parent benefit. But the claim that the government's budget is moving towards surplus certainly cannot be used to justify that or any other item of expenditure.

September 1998

THE 'IRON CHANCELLOR' AND GOVERNMENT SPENDING

In the last days of August and in early September 1999 there was much discussion of whether Gordon Brown really is an 'Iron Chancellor'. For, to the astonishment of many, on both the left and the right of politics, it appeared that a Labour Chancellor was producing public spending totals lower, as a share of national income, than his Conservative predecessors. Whether the surprise was appropriate can be decided by examining the history. But before doing so, it is necessary to be clear about what question is being asked, about whether it is a sensible question, and about the relevant facts.

Let us start by considering how the Chancellor has got into this situation. Government spending started to rise under the Conservatives; then control was regained by Kenneth Clarke when he was Chancellor. Gordon Brown has added to his inheritance, by reducing or abolishing allowances against tax, and by raising a wide variety of taxes. That accounts for part of the big fall in government borrowing. But there is another influence, quantitatively at least as important, which has both increased government tax revenue and reduced public spending as a share of national income. That is the economy itself: after slowing around the end of 1998 and the beginning of 1999, it accelerated again, and by autumn 1999 was showing strong growth in every sector and in most areas of the country.

Now, as the national income increases as a result of this boom, even if tax revenue and public spending stay unchanged, both the budget deficit and public spending automatically fall as a share of the (increased) national income. But, as the economy grows, taxes and public spending do not stay the same. Tax revenue goes up, and public spending goes up more slowly than planned. (Total public spending never falls – 'cuts' are invariably cuts in planned increases.)

It is clear why tax revenue goes up with national income. As income rises, people spend more. So they pay more VAT and more excise duty. And as more income is earned, of course more income tax is paid. Further, although inflation is by recent British standards low, it is not zero. Rising prices produce revenue for the Chancellor, for many taxes are proportional to the price of goods and some taxes – such as stamp duty on houses – move up in steps as house prices rise. Some parts of public expenditure also grow more slowly, and may even fall, as the economy booms. In particular, as more people are employed and as wages rise, less unemployment benefit is disbursed, and social security benefits paid are both fewer and smaller.

We can now see why a Chancellor cannot be judged as 'Iron' or its opposite by looking at public spending or public borrowing relative to national income in any one year. Both spending and borrowing are affected not just by the Chancellor's decisions, but by the behaviour of the economy. If the Chancellor is being judged on his ability to control spending and the budget deficit, he should be judged by his record over a number of years, including years of boom and years of sluggish growth.

Alternatively, he could in principle be judged by calculating what borrowing and spending would be if the economy were on trend – that is, growing at its average long-run rate. Unfortunately, doing that is not really possible. First, because the effect on government revenue and spending of national income deviating from trend is known only very roughly. Second, we never know what the trend is (for it can change); and we do not know precisely what it was (for there are errors of measurement and different [all defensible] ways of calculating the trend from the observed behaviour of national income).

So for a verdict on whether the present Chancellor is 'Iron' or not, we shall have to wait. Reaching one now would involve accepting the fallacy that one year's public spending to national income ratio is a meaningful number.

One more point must be made in conclusion. Those who are urging the Chancellor to spend more on the basis of the ratio are dangerous as well as misguided. Public spending has slowed because the economy is booming. When the boom ends, the elements that have led to the lower spending growth will increase, and make spending growth accelerate. If we spend more on the ever popular 'health and education' now, this spending will continue as the economy slows and the other elements of spending accelerate. So yet again we would have the familiar British problem of public spending surging out of control. Fallacies can be harmful as well as foolish.

December 1999

PART 6

MONETARY POLICY: THEORY

HIGH INTEREST RATES ARE BAD FOR THE ECONOMY, AND THE GOVERNMENT SHOULD REDUCE THEM FORTHWITH

The interest rate is a price. It is the price borrowers pay and the price savers receive. If we are to understand the consequences of a price – any price – being 'high' (which presumably means higher than average), we have to understand why it is high.

An example is useful. There is a rise in the price of bananas relative to other fruit. What will happen to sales of bananas? The answer is that we cannot say until we know why the price has risen.

It may have risen because there has been a cut-back in supply – as a result of a bad harvest. In this case, sales will fall, and the rise in price will have served to cut back the quantity demanded to the temporarily reduced amount available.

But the price could equally well have gone up because there was an increase in demand – because of change in tastes produced, say, by the discovery that bananas were exceptionally good for you. In this case, the increase in price accompanies an increase in sales – and if it persists will encourage increased investment in banana production.

The same argument applies to the interest rate. To understand the consequences of change in that price, just as in the case of the banana price, we have to understand the reason it has gone up. Traditionally, over more than 200 years, high interest rates have coincided with wars. They have been drawn up by demand to use resources in the present, rather than to invest them for future production. Less dramatic, but also clear, is the tendency for interest rates to rise and fall with the level of economic activity. Traditionally, rates have been pulled up by demand for resources. High interest rates are traditionally associated with high investment. They are the result of surges in the demand for funds to invest.

Why, then, the present concern to reduce interest rates to avoid harming investment? Partly, no doubt, they are the result of the quite reasonable desire of manufacturers (and all other borrowers) to see their costs fall. (It is perhaps a little surprising that calls by savers for higher interest rates are not equally common.) But also, and very important, is the reason interest rates are high. They have been pulled up by buoyant demand in the UK. And they have been pushed up by the authorities – the Bank of England acting at the behest of the government – to reduce money growth and thereby slow inflation.

That leads to two fresh questions. Which interest rates have they pulled up, and what was the alternative? The first entails long discussion, and is for another day. The second must be dealt with now.

If the authorities had not pushed up interest rates, what would have happened? Inflation would have accelerated, rising rapidly from the 5–6 per cent range and shooting into the teens. So that was the choice. Higher interest rates for a time, or accelerating inflation.

When that is understood, the fallacy involved in always complaining about high interest rates is clear. First, it matters why they are high – sometimes they are a sign of healthy economic growth. Second, choices cannot be evaluated one at a time; the available alternative has to be considered. If the authorities pushed down rates now, we would have spiralling inflation.

High interest rates are far from always bad; and at the moment, it would be folly to push rates down.

December 1988

INTERNATIONAL CAPITAL MOBILITY HAS INCREASED, SO GOVERNMENTS HAVE LITTLE CONTROL OVER ECONOMIC ACTIVITY

It is commonly claimed in broadcasts, in newspaper correspondence columns, and sometimes in articles on economics, that as a result of increased capital mobility the scope for a government to affect the course of the national economy is much reduced. Sometimes this is seen as good, sometimes bad; sometimes it is used as part of a case for European monetary union. And sometimes, and most worryingly, it is used as the basis of a case for restrictions on international capital movements.

But regardless of how the assertion is used, the fact is that it is totally wrong. International capital mobility can restrict a government's freedom of action. But it need not. Whether or not capital flows constrain government policy is a matter for the government's own choice. The circumstances under which they do constrain policy, and those in which they do not, are easily set out and contrasted.

Suppose first that a country is in a genuine fixed exchange rate system. The exchange rate of its currency is fixed against some other currency or currencies, and will not change. (A good example of such a situation is the relationship between English and Scottish pounds.) In such a setting, let the monetary authorities in one country try to ease monetary policy. An inevitable consequence of this is that short-term interest rates drop. When that happens, those who have funds in that country will move them to the other. There is, after all, no exchange risk, and a higher interest rate is on offer. Money will flow from one country to the other – tightening policy in the country which has eased, easing it in the country which has not. The overall effect on policy in the two countries cannot be specified in general; it depends on such factors as the relative size of the two countries, and on which is seen as 'the leader' in the conduct of monetary policy. But except in the special case where the country which has eased is the leader, and the other country follows, it is clear that in this set-up capital flows do constrain national monetary policies.

Now we look at the opposite case – of a freely floating exchange rate between the two economies. Once again, one country eases monetary policy and its interest rates fall. People try to move their capital. But this time the exchange rate is depressed by their doing so; indeed, it is highly likely to drop in anticipation. The exchange rate will in principle adjust until the expected return is the same in both currencies, and there will be no flow of money.

So in this second case, the monetary easing is *reinforced* by an exchange rate depreciation. It is not offset by a drain of money overseas.

Now, governments can choose whether to have a fixed exchange rate or a floating one. If they have a floating rate, then monetary policy is not constrained by international capital mobility. If they have a fixed exchange rate, then policy is so constrained. But there should be no complaint about that for it is a well-known consequence of fixed exchange rates.

In summary, capital flows can constrain national economic policies – but only if governments want them to.

September 1992

RISING BOND YIELDS WILL SLOW THE ECONOMY

In the spring and early summer of 1994, long-term interest rates – yields on government bonds – rose sharply, not just in Britain, but all around the world (although to different extents). Everywhere there was discussion of the consequences. In some countries it was argued that the rise meant the central bank need not tighten monetary policy to slow the economy. In others, there were fears the rise would prolong recessions which previously had appeared to be ending. In any event, there seemed to be a consensus that the rise would affect the economy, so as to slow down or reverse economic growth to at least a modest extent.

There was also some rather limited discussion of why the rise had occurred, but curiously no one linked it with discussion of the consequence of the rise. That is a pity, for if they had they might have reached rather different conclusions.

The return on long-term government bonds has two parts – the real rate of interest and the expected rate of inflation over the life of the bond. The two sum to make the interest rate on the bond. The first component is the return in real terms that lenders receive. It is the payment they get for abstaining from consumption now, the increase in future purchasing power they obtain for lending out their money rather than spending it. This return is unaffected by inflation. It could, indeed, actually be paid in physical units of whatever the money borrowed is used to produce. Usually it is not, but that is only because it is convenient in a money-using economy to be paid in money rather than, say, in bicycles or wine. The return reflects a genuine increase in purchasing power as a result of having saved and lent out the saving. Borrowers are willing to pay that return because they judge that, by borrowing and spending, they get a return which compensates them for the payments they made to the lender. Thus the real rate is determined by the supply of savings and the demand for funds to invest. If people become more willing to save, the real rate will fall; and vice versa. As for borrowers, if they see more or better investment projects, they will bid up the real rate; however, should attractive investment projects become more rare, the real rate will fall.

In other words, the real rate of interest is a price which moves in response to changes in the desire to consume now relative to consuming later, and in response to changes in demand for funds to invest.

What about expected inflation? Lenders will want compensation for any fall in the value of money they think will occur over the period of the loan. Otherwise, the money they get back in the future would not buy what it could when they lent it out – they could end up worse off as a result of saving. Should lenders not demand this compensation, borrowers would enjoy a windfall by borrowing at a negative real interest rate.

Where does this lead for the rise in bond yields? They can have risen for two reasons. Either the real rate or expected inflation has gone up (or a bit of both). What are the consequences for the economy?

If real rates have gone up, there is a change in demand relative to supply for consumption goods or investment goods. There is no reason why this should affect the *total* of economic activity. It would certainly affect the *composition* of output, and there might be a temporary dip in the total while resources are moved from one area of activity to another. But there is no reason why such a rise should have more than a very temporary effect on economic activity.

What about expected inflation? If expected inflation increases, people will switch from assets which are vulnerable to inflation into ones which offer some form of protection against it. They will, for example, switch out of currency and bank accounts which do not pay interest. What effect will this have on the economy? To the extent that it is noticeable, it will boost demand, for there will be an increase – perhaps temporary – in the demand for the goods. In summary, there is no reason for an increase in bond yields to slow the economy. The fallacy arises from forgetting that a bond yield is a price. One can never discuss the consequences of a price change without knowing why it has happened. Prices change in response to changes in the economy. Only when it is known what these changes are can the consequences of the resulting price movement sensibly be discussed. Changes in bond yields – or in any other price – have effects on the economy which depend on the cause of the price change. Prices reflect what is happening in the economy. Forgetting that can lead to accepting as true the fallacy that changing bond yields affect economic activity. Treating other prices that way can also lead to accepting many other fallacies; but those are for another day.

October 1994

A BOOST TO DEMAND FROM MONETARY POLICY WILL HELP GROWTH

For some years in the 1960s and 1970s British governments acted as if they could expand demand and thus get *and keep* unemployment down and the level of economic activity up. That policy was renounced by James (now Lord) Callaghan in a famous speech to the Labour Party Conference but it is now re-appearing. The revival is being led by, of all countries, Germany – which never followed it in the years when Britain, along with other countries, did.

Indeed, Germany may well be reviving the error in still more virulent form, for the German government seems to believe that by forcing monetary easing on the European Central Bank it will boost growth, not just the level of income as was previously believed.

What is wrong with the belief? Most basic, and running all through the fallacy in various guises, is a confusion between real and nominal variables. Real variables are things like goods and services, the number of workers employed, and so forth; and thus aggregates of them – national income and employment respectively – are *real* variables. Nominal variables are money variables – the general level of prices, as measured by a price index, and the amount of money in circulation, to name two important nominal variables.

Easing monetary conditions is usually thought of as the central bank lowering interest rates; but a by-product of this is inevitably, an increase in the growth rate of money. When central banks lower interest rates, they buy securities in the financial markets, thus raising their price and lowering the yield. And to buy them they issue money.

So the German government is saying printing money will raise the growth rate of national income, the aggregate of goods and services produced in the economy. That is wrong. For it means that by printing more pieces of paper – or not even bothering to do that, but just increasing bank deposits – the economy's rate of growth would increase. If that were true, surely it would have been tried before.

Printing money has been tried before. The consequence has not, however, been a higher growth rate. Rather, when countries have eased money to a substantial extent they have just ended up with higher inflation. So the 'theory' does not fit the facts.[1]

Initially when monetary policy is eased demand expands. The fall in interest rates induces more people to borrow, some for consumption and some for investment. This increases the demand for goods. For a time people are willing to supply goods to meet this extra demand – for they can raise the prices of their goods, and thus seem to

---

1 Evidence on the relationship between money and inflation can be found in an essay by Forrest Capie in *Money, Prices and the Real Economy*, 1998, edited by G. E. Wood, and published jointly by Edward Elgar and the Institute of Economic Affairs.

be better off. But it emerges sooner or later that all prices have gone up. For *every* producer has raised prices, so no one is better off in *real* terms. The gain is purely in money terms. The incentive to supply more at the higher price has thus gone. The price of inputs has gone up, as has the price of what producers consume, so they are no better off than before. They are getting more money, but each unit of money buys less. The monetary expansion thus produces at most a temporary boost to output; after a time, even this is reversed, and output falls back to around its previous level.[2]

Hence, we can see that the belief that a monetary expansion boosts output is fallacious, and also why it is fallacious. It came about because a boost to demand by monetary easing can raise output for a time. It does so, though, only so long as people are fooled that a nominal change is a real one. When they see through the nominal change, the change in output reverses.

How could this fallacy lead to the belief that monetary easing can actually raise growth? When the monetary easing takes place, output starts to rise: but this is a temporary change in output above its long-run trend. The economy ultimately reverts to its trend. Those who think monetary easing will raise the growth rate, and thus solve (some of) the economic problems of continental Europe,

---

2   For a time it was believed that a monetary expansion, and the associated higher rate of inflation, could produce a sustained increase in the level of output (not, notice, in its rate of growth). This belief and its collapse is documented in a paper by Robert H. Rasche, in G. E. Wood (ed.), op. cit.

are confused twice over. They are not distinguishing between real and nominal changes, and they are confusing a temporary and one-off boost to the level of output with a change in the economy's long-run rate of growth.

To conclude, then, the belief that the European Central Bank can increase Europe's growth rate by cutting interest rates and increasing the supply of euros is fallacious. There might be a boost to the level of output – but this would reverse, and the euro area would be left with higher inflation. There would be no beneficial effects on the economy's growth rate at all – and, indeed, there might be harm through the effects of inflation. Real and nominal variables should not be confused. If they are, many fallacious beliefs follow, and some of them have seriously damaging consequences for the economy.

March 1999

IT IS SENSIBLE TO JUDGE PAST DECISIONS IN THE LIGHT OF CURRENT INFORMATION

Recently a report was published which claimed that the British government was paying 'too much' for its borrowing. What exactly was meant by saying that the government was paying 'too much' and, if it was doing so, does it matter?

Some years ago the government issued debt with (for example) 30 years before it was due to be redeemed, at an interest rate of (to choose a round number) 10 per cent per annum. But, as can be seen from the markets where such debt is traded, 30-year debt could now be sold on a yield of (to choose another round number) 5 per cent per annum. Hence, the claim is that old debt is 'costing too much'.

Before we examine that claim, it is useful to digress for a moment to consider whether, supposing it is correct, it matters. The reason the question is worth asking is that most British government debt is held by or on behalf of (through pension funds, for example) British citizens. Hence the interest is paid by taking money from some citizens (by taxes) and giving it to another group. It is a pure 'internal transfer'. Moreover, quite a few of the people who pay the taxes receive the interest, either now or, through their pensions, later. Since the interest is just being shifted around within the country, does the interest rate on the debt matter?

In fact, it clearly increases taxes. Taxes affect people's decisions to save, invest, work and consume. They distort them away from what they would have been without the taxes. Hence there is a cost to high interest payments on government debt, and if the rate on the debt is unnecessarily high, it is indeed grounds for criticism because of its costly consequences.

To consider whether an avoidable mistake has been made, we need to think about why interest rates have fallen so much – in our example, not so far from what has actually happened, halved. The answer lies in what determines interest rates. There are basically three, quite different, kinds of factor at work, each influencing one of the interest rate's three components.

These three components are the real rate of interest, the risk premium and expected inflation. When people work and spend, they receive and then spend money – but what they are concerned with are the goods the money buys. The real rate of interest measures the command over goods and services that borrowers are giving up when borrowing, and that lenders receive by lending. That is the rate which equalises the demand to borrow with the supply of lending.

These borrowing and lending transactions are (almost invariably) carried out in money terms, so to the real rate of interest expected inflation is added. Lenders demand it, and borrowers pay it, because they were willing to borrow at the real rate it implies. Finally is added a risk premium, to compensate for possibility of default on the loan, and to allow for errors in forecasting inflation.

Which of these things has changed to lower the interest rate on British government debt? Plainly, whatever has happened to the other two, inflation has come down – not just actual inflation, but expected inflation. Giving the Bank of England a mandate to achieve a particular, and reasonably low, inflation rate will have stabilised inflation expectations around that target rate. This is not because the Bank will hit that rate all the time – or even at all. Rather it is because the Bank has the tools to hit that rate on average; and it is the average over a period of years that matters for long-term bond contracts. So at least one reason long-term interest rates have fallen is that expected inflation has fallen.

So, having argued that the fall in inflation expectations has been important for the behaviour of interest rates it is now clear it is only possible to say that 'too much' was paid to borrow if it was clear – or likely – at the time the borrowing took place that inflation was going to fall. Was it? Two points must be made here. First, if it had been *clear*, then interest rates would have been lower than they were: buyers of bonds would have pushed rates down. So there must, at the least, have been *some* risk of inflation staying where it was or going higher. Second, could anyone at the time have anticipated the mandate that was given to the Bank of England? Surely not. It was a surprise to most observers when it happened.

While it is true that had we known some years ago what we know now, interest rates would be lower on government debt, we did not have the same information in the past as we now have. One can learn from comparing what was expected with what has actually happened. But it is only sensible to judge whether mistakes were made on that basis if there was not a change in relevant circumstances between actions and outcomes. Only if that condition is granted can we judge past decisions in the light of current information.

June 2000

PART 7

MONETARY POLICY: PRACTICE

THE BANK OF ENGLAND SHOULD
RESCUE A FAILED OR FAILING BANK

A common fallacy, given new life at the start of the financial crisis in Britain by the failure of Northern Rock, is that a central bank has a duty, in its role as lender of last resort, to rescue a bank which has failed or is just about to fail. In fact, central banks *never* should do that and seldom *could* do so. Claiming that they should misunderstands the central bank's responsibility as 'lender of last resort'.

This task (whose naming, interestingly, is usually credited to Sir Francis Baring in 1797) arises because central banks now have a monopoly over the note issue, and of the supply of deposits at the central bank – two ultimate means of settlement in a monetary system and the medium of exchange in which confidence remains after it has been lost in all others. If confidence is lost in central bank money, the whole monetary system breaks down.

Banks hold only a small portion of reserves against their liabilities. They take deposits, and lend out the majority of them. Only a small fraction is retained as cash or its equivalent, a deposit at the central bank. Thus it is possible – though unlikely – that a bank will run out of cash if withdrawals exceed deposits. A bank's first recourse in such an event is to borrow from other banks. Usually it can do so without difficulty, for one bank's excess of withdrawals over deposits implies an excess of deposits over withdrawals for the rest of the system.

But occasionally this has not been possible. Such episodes usually happened immediately after a bank failed – as a result, say, of incompetence, bad luck or even fraud. Depositors in the bank usually lost some or all of their deposits. Seeing depositors at the failed bank losing money, depositors at other banks sometimes went to their banks (in some haste) and, as a precaution, withdrew their deposits. When this happened, the entire system could quickly be drained of cash, and would fail. That would be disastrous, for it would wipe out a large part of a country's money stock, and thus cause a severe recession. In those circumstances, the central bank acted as a lender of last resort. It lent cash, on the security of treasury bills and bills of exchange, to the banking system. The liquidity of the system was then restored and, as experience of several such episodes has shown, so was confidence in the banking system.

The Bank of England acted as a lender of last resort in the way described several times in the 19th century. Walter Bagehot (in his book, *Lombard Street*, first published in 1873) is often credited with persuading the Bank to act in that way. But the Bank had so acted several times before his book appeared. What Bagehot did was to urge the Bank to make plain in advance that it stood ready to act as a lender of last resort whenever necessary. He argued that knowledge the Bank was willing to provide cash (in exchange for security) would itself help to prevent panic demands for cash emerging.

That description of the role of lender of last resort makes plain the role is narrow and precisely defined. If people flee with their deposits from one bank because they fear it to be unsound and about to fall, there is *no need* for lender-of-last-resort action if they flee not to cash but, as is more likely today, to another bank (as, for example, when Continental Illinois Bank in the USA was about to fail). In such circumstances, the system is not drained of cash; the cash is simply redistributed.

The 'last resort' role, and the analysis and evidence which explain and justify it, need never involve bailing out an insolvent bank. Not only is such action unnecessary; it is also undesirable, and usually for the central bank impossible. It is undesirable because if depositors know that banks will always be bailed out, they will go to the bank which, by taking the greatest risks can, at any rate for a time, pay the greatest returns to depositors and shareholders. For their part, banks will have few incentives to prudence, and will go for the greatest returns almost regardless of risk. Bailing out banks would reward reckless behaviour.

Moreover, the central bank could seldom do it. Bailing out a bank requires an injection of new capital. Central banks do not have large balance sheets. They do not have the capital to bail out any but the tiniest of financial institutions. Hence it is the French taxpayer (via the French government), not the Banque de France, that is bailing out Crédit Lyonnais.

To summarise, the lender of last resort is concerned with the stability of the monetary system, not that of individual banks. If for some reason a bank becomes insolvent, it should be allowed to fail. Doing otherwise not only does not serve any good purpose: rather it serves a bad one, by rewarding failure.

It is not clear whether post-crash regulation is well designed in view of that. Banks are being compelled to hold more capital. If they behave as regulators demand, and something goes wrong, they may well claim that it is not their fault. Again, failure may be rewarded by bail out. Post-crisis regulation should be concerned to ensure that banks can fail in an orderly manner and without causing widespread disruption, not with the unachievable objective of making banks failure-proof.[1]

June 1995
(Updated April 2014)

---

1 These issues are examined in Forrest Capie and Geoffrey Wood, *Do we need regulation of bank capital? Some evidence from the UK*, IEA, 2013.

MONETARY AND EXCHANGE-RATE POLICY CAN BE CONDUCTED INDEPENDENTLY OF EACH OTHER

The European Central Bank (ECB) is charged with conducting monetary policy for the whole euro area. Its mandate is to deliver low inflation (defined as in the range of 0–2 per cent per annum) and, subject to that, to 'support the policies' of the euro-area governments. Presumably that means to dampen recessions; but, whatever meaning attaches to the phrase, that task is subordinated to the delivery of low inflation. So far all is clear. But then along comes German minister Oskar Lafontaine (now resigned), talking of currency zones; of stabilising the euro against the dollar and yen, or, if the USA does not get involved, stabilising the euro against the yen alone.

There are of course questions about that policy – such as whether a stable yen is of any benefit to Japan at the moment. But be that as it may, there is a more fundamental problem – and one which should worry every resident in the euro area who wants stable prices – with such plans. The problem is that monetary policy and exchange-rate policy cannot be conducted independently of each other.

Suppose first that the ECB has accomplished its task, and is delivering inflation at (for example) an average rate of 1 per cent per annum.

Further, for simplicity, suppose that it is generally expected that inflation will stay around that level. Now let there be a monetary expansion in the USA, such that inflation is expected to rise – not at an horrendous rate, but a rate that the USA has experienced in recent memory, 4 per cent a year, for example.

If the euro and the dollar were initially stable against one another, they would be so no longer. It would be clear that in the future each dollar was going to buy fewer goods than had previously been expected, while expectations about the future purchasing power of the euro would not change. Accordingly, the dollar would start to weaken relative to the euro.

This weakening would not be smooth. The markets in which currencies are traded are fast-moving. No one wants to hold a currency the value of which they expect to fall in the future, so they sell it now. Thus expectations of a declining dollar would lead in the first instance to a sharp drop in its value. But goods prices do not change as fast. Hence the euro price of US goods (priced in dollars) falls (because the dollar has fallen) until the dollar price catches up as a result of the US inflation. This immediately puts pressure on the producers of all euro-area goods which compete with goods produced in the USA. Whether they are trying to export to the USA or to sell in the euro area in competition with US imports is immaterial. Competition will temporarily increase. What is to be done? One possibility would be to inflate in the euro area. This would of course weaken the euro just as US inflation had weakened the dollar. But the ECB is committed to low inflation, so there will not be a deliberate inflation. There is, however, a policy which is sometimes supposed to be an alternative – foreign-exchange intervention.

By that is meant the monetary authorities buying (or selling) their currency in the foreign-exchange markets, so as to appreciate (or depreciate) its value. In the present case, the objective would be to depreciate the euro, so euros would be sold in the foreign-exchange market. That would work all too well.

For it would be increasing the supply of money just as surely as the ECB's easing monetary policy would be increasing the supply of money. The only significant difference between foreign-exchange intervention and domestic monetary policy is that their impact effects are in different markets. The first affects the foreign exchanges, the second has its first impact on domestic short-term interest rates. Beyond that stage, however, they are just different ways of doing the same thing. They both change the supply of currency. Hence an attempt to stop the euro appreciating would entail easing monetary policy, by one route or another, in the euro area.

That leads us to the proposal for currency stabilisation. Again, the only instrument to achieve this is monetary policy, carried out by either domestic money-market operations or by operations in the foreign-exchange market.

Hence the ECB would have to switch from its present objective, low inflation, to a new objective, a stable exchange rate.

There is one minor qualification to be made. It is possible to carry out 'sterilised intervention' – selling the currency (for example) on the foreign exchanges, and buying back a like amount in the domestic money markets, so that the total stock of money is unchanged. But that would be ineffective in changing the exchange rate.

To conclude, there is no way round the interdependence of exchange rates and monetary policy. A recommendation to stabilise the euro is inevitably a recommendation to give up control of inflation. Recommendations to allow a euro depreciation are recommendations to encourage euro inflation. Any sensible central bank would resist such advice, and not try to achieve two inconsistent objectives at once.

June 1999

SCOTLAND SHOULD BE
REPRESENTED ON THE MPC

For many years now there have been complaints from Scots that the Bank of England is conducting monetary policy inappropriately, not taking account of economic conditions in Scotland. The remedy then proposed is that Scotland should have a 'representative' on the Monetary Policy Committee (MPC). It used to be a long-term aim of the SNP that Scotland, when independent, should join the euro area. The fallacy behind the first proposed remedy is set out first, and that behind the longer-term objective second.

The Bank of England has a mandate to control inflation (currently as measured by the CPI, and previously as measured by the RPI) and to keep it in a fairly narrow range close to but above zero. (There are various qualifications to that – there is an implication that a greater deviation would be acceptable if a satisfactory explanation were given – but the basic mandate is as described.) Now, inflation is a comparatively new term for a year-after-year rise in the price of goods and services. Such a rise in prices used to be called a *fall in the purchasing power of money*. The two terms plainly mean the same thing; if prices in general have gone up, then money will buy less. But the old-fashioned term is useful in the present context.

The reason is that it reminds us that the same money is used in Scotland and in England. The Bank of England's mandate is therefore to control the 'purchasing power of money' over the whole area. It controls it not for London, not for Birmingham, not for Glasgow (or indeed for Southend or Aberdeen either) but for the average of the whole of the United Kingdom. For that is the area over which are measured the prices which go into producing the inflation rate.

Put another way, what is being controlled is an average inflation rate for the whole country. Some prices might rise faster than the average in London, and some slower than that in, say, Glasgow or Edinburgh. But from the point of view of the mandate given to the Monetary Policy Committee of the Bank of England, that is beside the point. And more important – much more important, lest anyone get the notion that changing the mandate to take account of 'regional differences' would be a good idea – so long as the UK uses one money, the Bank of England can only control the average purchasing power across the country. It uses an interest rate which applies across the country, to control monetary conditions and thus the value of money. It is just not possible to set one interest rate for England and another for Scotland so long as both countries use the same currency.

Now, the Scots might accept that but still complain that, given the state of the Scottish economy, monetary policy has been set too tight for the UK of which Scotland is a part. That is a logically reasonable complaint. But it does not fit the facts. For the inflation target is being hit. Inflation is running only slightly below target, so it cannot be maintained that weak demand in Scotland is holding prices back to such an extent as to keep UK inflation too low.

Scotland's problem – if a problem it has over this – can be solved only by having its own currency.[1]

What of the argument that an independent Scotland should join the euro? That policy would create exactly the same problem. True, so long as Scotland created a central bank before joining the euro area, the governor of that bank would be on the council of the European Central Bank (ECB). But that governor would not be there to represent Scotland's interests and to argue for a monetary policy that suited Scotland. Rather the task would be to help produce a monetary policy which delivered price stability for the whole of the euro area. It would be a 'large-scale' (so to speak) version of the task now facing the Bank of England. It would be no more appropriate for the ECB to focus policy on one region than it is for the Bank of England, and, indeed, no more possible.

Supporters of European monetary union are sometimes given to using the slogan 'One Market, One Money.' It would be more useful, as well as more meaningful and correct, to say 'One Money, One Monetary Policy.'

---

1 It is also a fallacy that Scotland could not use sterling if she were to vote for independence. This fallacy is examined on pages 163–166.

The Federal Reserve System in the United States reinforces this point. The US central bank, the Federal Reserve, is in fact a network of Federal Reserve Banks, scattered over the country and each having certain banking responsibilities in its region. But these banks do not conduct monetary policy for their own regions, and nor do their respective presidents, when they gather together to set monetary policy at the headquarters of the Federal Reserve in Washington, argue that national policy should be set in line with the particular interests of their region. They do bring expertise about their local economies; but this is used to help inform a judgement on national monetary policy, not to produce a monetary policy for their regions.

In summary, so long as Scotland and England have the same money they must have the same monetary policy. And so long as the inflation rate is within target, neither Scotland nor any other region can complain that the influence of economic conditions in their region on the economy as a whole is being neglected.

September 2000

GOVERNMENTS CAN CONTROL WHO
USES THEIR COUNTRY'S MONEY

At first glance this seems scarcely a fallacy. It is something people rarely think about. But just recently the idea has become prominent, as almost all politicians opposed to Scottish independence claim not only that an independent Scotland would have no say in Bank of England monetary policy decisions, but that it would not be 'allowed' to use the pound sterling. The belief does not, incidentally, occur only in this context. Other examples are discussed below.

When the leader of the Scottish Nationalist Party was first asked about an independent Scotland's monetary arrangements, he said that Scotland would join the euro zone. Either because that became economically less attractive or he saw how it compromised the independence of small countries, he retreated from that idea, and said Scotland would use sterling. Here he was promptly rebuffed.

On pages 159–162, it has been shown how under present monetary arrangements a 'Scottish' vote on the Monetary Policy Committee (MPC) does not make sense, as that group of experts is trying to conduct monetary policy for the UK as a whole, not a collection of regional representatives. They aim to achieve roughly stable prices for the whole of the UK, and focus on various measures of the general level of prices for the whole of the UK.

If Scotland continued to use sterling *with the consent of the government of the remainder of the UK*, that consent would surely be based on Scottish acceptance that the policy objective continued as before, or even switched to a price index based solely on prices in the remainder of the UK. In either case appointments to the MPC would continue to be made on the same basis as before, and only if a price index including prices in Scotland were targeted would Scotland have an influence on policy decisions. And of course the influence would be indirect, and not exerted through discussion and voting at the MPC. (That, incidentally, would under present rules continue to be the case if someone resident in Scotland were to be appointed to the MPC.)

There is, however, another way in which Scotland could continue to use sterling. Suppose you make a trip to, say, Jersey or Guernsey, you would find the bank notes in use familiar. (The one obvious novelty would be the survival of the one-pound note.) Look more closely, and you would see that the notes are issued not by the Bank of England but by the respective governments of each island, and signed by a senior officer of each island's government.

How can they do this? Because they hold substantial reserves of liquid sterling assets, so that should anyone demand 'Bank of England sterling', it can be supplied readily. Both islands are operating currency boards – systems found elsewhere in the world too, and in which one country uses the money of another, but has no say in how monetary policy is conducted. It just automatically follows the monetary policy of the money-issuing country. Such systems have collapsed from time to time, for they require sense on the part of the currency board country. This means not allowing banks in the country to lend wildly with few reserves and not themselves borrowing amounts so large that in times of even modest stress there would be doubts about their ability to repay. But they have proved very durable in both the 19th and 20th centuries, and have continued to be so in the present century.

Scotland could follow that course, and the government of the remainder of the UK would not have the power to stop it.

What about the Bank of England? A crucial part of a central bank's role is to act as lender of last resort. This means that if there is sudden demand for cash made on the banking system, such that the system as a whole does not have enough, then the Bank of England supplies cash in exchange for securities of various sorts (both government securities and private ones) from the banks. Is there any reason the Bank of England would not do that for the Scottish banking system should it be necessary?

Unless it took securities it was not completely sure of, implicitly believing that the institution it took them from would not go bankrupt or that if it did it would be bailed out, there would be no reason for additional caution in its dealings with the Scottish banking system. And if the Bank of England did choose to relax its lending standards in such a crisis, it could quite reasonably relax them a little less for Scottish banks than for English ones. If Scottish banks were told the rules in advance, they could play the game with a little more caution. And cautious banking did use to be a Scottish tradition.

Turning to another possibility worth noting, can governments force people to use their money if the people do not want to? By coercion it can largely be done – although US dollars were used in the Soviet Union despite the wishes of its government. And there are numerous examples of a money being replaced by some foreign one if most of the private sector wishes to transact in it. All transactions not coerced to be otherwise – the payment of taxes maybe – would by private, voluntary, sometimes implicit, agreement take place in foreign not in domestic money.

To conclude, it would be irrational for the remainder of the UK to try to stop an independent Scotland using the pound sterling. And, perhaps more important, it would be impossible as well. Governments sometimes have less power than they believe.

April 2014

PART 8

COST, PRICE AND VALUE

OIL COMPANIES HAVE BEEN ROBBING THE PUBLIC BY RAISING PRICES WHEN THEY HAVE INVENTORIES BOUGHT AT PREVIOUS, LOWER, PRICES

The above complaint against oil companies is an example – an example motivated by dramatic price movements – of a common and durable fallacy. The fallacy is to think that prices should be based on historic cost – what something used to cost, rather than an opportunity cost – what it is worth now.

The example of oil is a convenient one to use to analyse why prices should be determined by opportunity cost. Suppose oil companies hold stocks of oil, bought at a low price. The price of oil then rises. What if they sell all their stocks at the old price, and do not raise prices until new stocks have to be purchased?

Suppose first that oil prices rise but never fall. Every time there is a price rise, when oil companies have sold their stocks, they are unable to replace them without borrowing, running down assets or raising more capital.

If they behaved like this every time the price rose, what would happen? Their borrowing would rise without limit – of course, well before that, they would be unable to borrow and oil production would halt. Alternatively, they would run out of assets and oil production would halt. What of raising new capital? Does that help them out? Yet again the answer is 'no'. For who would invest in them if it were guaranteed that some of the investment would be lost whenever the price of raw materials went up?

In other words, under the assumption that oil prices can go up but not down, selling stocks at historic rather than opportunity cost guarantees that oil companies go out of business and that oil production ceases.

But of course oil prices both rise and fall. Does this affect the conclusion that stocks should be sold at opportunity cost? In this case, if companies always price at opportunity cost, they raise prices when raw material prices rise and lower them when they fall – thus making a 'windfall profit' when prices rise and a 'windfall loss' when they fall. In such a case, would pricing at historic cost not be quite satisfactory? For retail prices would still rise and fall, with a lag depending on how long it took for stocks to run down, and the viability of oil production would not be threatened. The answer is that even then historic cost pricing would be a dangerous error. Why? Because there is always the possibility that a change in oil price would not reverse, or that the trend was upwards. The contraction or extinction of the industry would again be threatened.

Pricing at opportunity cost has no harmful effects on the consumer in the short term, and avoids the threat of the industry collapsing. A similar analysis can be set out for falls in price – except that now, if pricing is at historic rather than opportunity cost, the industry expands without limit!

To conclude, then, pricing at opportunity cost produces efficient resource allocation. Pricing at historic cost can produce the collapse of industries whose products people want and will pay for. Opportunity cost pricing is sensible and historic cost pricing foolish.

February 1991

CUTTING OUT THE MIDDLEMAN
BRINGS DOWN PRICES

Sometimes in advertisements consumers are exhorted to deal directly with the manufacturer, and by thus 'cutting out the middleman' save themselves money by buying the goods at a lower price. Middlemen are sometimes bracketed with 'racketeers' as people who raise prices to consumers – and often depress them to producers – as people, in fact, whose activities serve no good purpose. These advertisements and these criticisms (certainly so far as middlemen go) are misleading, for 'middlemen' serve a very useful purpose indeed.

There is an article, very famous to economists, called *On the Nature of the Firm*. In that article Ronald Coase (a Nobel Prize winner in Economics) asked why firms exist. Why, he asked, is each stage of production not carried out by independent contractors? The answer lies in the existence of transaction costs. Firms group together the parts of the production process which are best carried out by one organisation, rather than by a series of separate ones dealing with each other in the market-place.

This is why different industries are integrated – have production stages 'under one roof' – to different extents and also why firms in an industry can display different degrees of integration at different times. Different, and changing, technologies explain this observation; for they require different degrees of integration.

Realising this shows that the very definition of a middleman is not so straightforward as it seems. As technologies change, sometimes an activity – delivering the good, say – will be done by the firm, and sometimes a separate contractor. Surely it is ludicrous to describe the activity disparagingly, as parasitic, on some occasions, and as desirably productive on others, simply as a result of change in the ownership of the organisation which executes it.

'Middlemen' serve an economic purpose. They take the good from one place to another. They may buy large quantities and sell in smaller. They may hold inventories, so that the goods are continually available even though being produced only from time to time – in batches by the contractor or seasonally by Nature.

If the middleman is cut out, someone will have to do the job or jobs he did. And they will expect to be paid for doing so. Those who say, 'buy direct and cut out the middleman', are actually saying 'buy direct and use us as a middleman'. Unless they are willing to make losses, they must be paid for that activity. They are paid by higher prices or lower quality, offering smaller ranges, by insisting on buying in larger quantities, and no doubt by other means also. If there is not a 'middleman', all that has changed is that the task is done within the firm rather than by a separate organisation. 'Cutting out the middleman' effects no savings; for the middleman's work must still be done. Middlemen serve a useful function, and cannot be costlessly eliminated.

April 1992

FARMERS SHOULD BE PAID THEIR
COSTS OF PRODUCTION

A fine example of this fallacy is to be found on the Fairtrade Foundation website.

> '...companies that trade in Fairtrade products in the UK...
> [should] ... pay at least a price to producers the covers the
> costs of sustainable production: the Fairtrade Minimum
> Price.'

But many other examples could be found.

The idea that if something is costly to produce then it is valuable pervades many aspects of life – even education, where now and again it is argued that someone deserves a good mark, or even a good degree, because he has 'worked hard'. But although all-pervasive, and indeed long-established, the belief is wrong.

When a person buys a good he is seeking to make himself (or the person for whom it is bought) as well off as possible, *given what he can afford to spend*. People thus look to see what provides the best value for their expenditure. How do we judge that?

What we look at is the satisfaction the good gives. In finding this out, people ask a whole range of questions. Is the good attractive? Is it reliable? Is it long-lasting? Or, perhaps, is the taste pleasing? Or, is it comfortable? The range can be added to considerably; which questions are appropriate depend of course on the nature of the good.

But every one of these questions is in essence a specific form of 'What will this good do for me?' The questions are concerned with the *satisfaction* the consumption of the good provides. This satisfaction is (in general) independent of the effort and resources that have gone into producing the good. Consider the example of tomatoes. Suppose that at the same time in the year, tomatoes could be obtained from Scotland – by growing them in hot-houses which had been insulated and heated; or from, say, Morocco, where they grow in the open air with no attention except that needed to pick them. Would we pay more for the Scottish ones because they had been produced with more difficulty?

It is unlikely. Indeed, quite often there is no way the consumer can know – the goods are side by side, identical in all respects from the point of view of the satisfaction they give. If the information is absent it cannot affect the price!

There may be the occasional exception to this rule – people may value more something that is made by hand rather than by machine. But even here, what is usually valued is not being hand-made, but a *result* of that. Every example of the good will be slightly different from every other one – that is often an attraction.

Now, does this mean that costs of production do not matter at all? Of course it does not, but they do not matter for price. What they determine is whether the good continues to be supplied. Consider again the example of our valiant but misguided Scottish tomato grower. His costs of production will exceed the price at which he can sell his tomatoes. He will lose money, and leave the market, unless he both gets satisfaction from supplying the good and has some other source of income to allow continued subsidy of his tomato growing.

The point is a simple one. The conclusion that costs of production are irrelevant to price, and that price is determined by what consumers are willing to pay, follows directly from observing that people consume goods for the satisfaction they give. But although simple, it has widespread application, and ignoring it would lead to foolish decisions and to waste and misallocation of resources.

Take education. If someone is given a good degree because he has 'worked hard', think of the implication for a prospective employer. He will not be able to tell whether a prospective employee is a hard-working dunce or actually understands the subject of the degree. The qualification would give no information.

More generally, if goods were valued for the resources they used up rather than the satisfaction they gave, resources would deliberately be used wastefully so as to increase the price of the output. This would diminish the supply of other goods that could be provided. It would be behaviour that created scarcity where there could have been abundance.

To conclude, the value of what has been used to produce a good – whether what has been used is effort or other types of scarce resources – is irrelevant to what the good is worth. Whether people will pay what it cost to produce is important, but important for determining if the good continues to be supplied. Goods are worth what people will pay for them, and that does not depend on their cost of production.

June 1994
(Updated April 2014)

PART 9

LABOUR MARKETS

THEY'RE NOT WELL PAID.
THEY SHOULD GET A LIVING WAGE

We often hear when a group of lower-paid workers goes on strike that they 'deserve more', that they 'need a living wage'. There is now something called the 'London Living Wage', above the minimum wage set by central government and supported on the grounds that the cost of living is higher in London than in the rest of the country. Although certainly well-meant, these ideas would end up making most people – particularly the low-paid – worse off.

It is useful to make the starting point of the discussion clear. Suppose that at the existing wage rate there are coming forward for work just the number of workers required, and that they work normal hours (that is, neither overtime nor short time on an average week) to meet demand for the product. These workers get together, and thinking that they are not paid a 'living wage', go on strike.

It is possible the employers could increase their wages; the employers might be monopolists, or they might be receiving a subsidy from the taxpayer to cover their costs. In any event, as a result of the increase in wages employers do not want to employ any fewer workers.

So the same number of workers is wanted, but higher wages are being paid. As this will lead to more workers applying, some – the *least able* – will be rejected. (It must be emphasised that this argument does not assume that people work only for money – what it assumes is that pay is one of the factors people are interested in.)

As a result of the wage increase some of the people who were previously in jobs are unemployed; and some of the people who have taken their place have come from other jobs where they are worth more, but are paid less because their employer is neither a monopolist nor subsidised to pay them more than the value they contribute to output.

This second effect, the diversion of more skilled workers, lowers the output of the economy. So we have more unemployment and less output as a result of 'paying a living wage'. This may seem a harsh conclusion. It is not. What it does is remind us that there are foolish ways as well as sensible ways to solve a problem.

In this case, the problem is that there are some jobs which are worth having done only at wages which society regards as too low – they provide too poor a standard of living. But paying more for these jobs makes things worse.

It is also worth looking at the case where the employer decides to pay the workers more, but cannot pass on this cost increase to either his customers or the general body of taxpayers.

The increased labour costs cannot be absorbed without increasing prices for, if they were, other factors of production – raw materials and capital – could be paid less than they would earn elsewhere. The employer could not just cut back what he paid for raw materials; if he did, no one would sell to him. And capital would end up earning less than it could elsewhere. This would lead to it being employed elsewhere. His only course is to charge more for his products, sell less, and employ fewer workers. Again unemployment rises.

What should, then, be done? What to do is to pay people money from general taxes. The people who receive this money can then go out and earn more without losing what they have already received.

If we simply decide to pay people more for their work without regard to what they produce, we will end up unable to pay them at all. Pay should be separate from social provisions – otherwise resources are wasted, and when that happens the poor are the first to suffer.

October 1989
(Updated April 2014)

WOMEN SHOULD GET LONGER
PAID MATERNITY LEAVE

There is a long tradition of different groups arguing that they deserve special treatment in the jobs market. This is one of the examples. It is quite understandable that women should ask for, and get, special leave from work after giving birth to children. But forgetting that there are costs arising from that does them, and everybody else, no good at all.

It embodies the fallacy that workers are employed regardless of what they cost. If anyone were to assert boldly that employers did not care about their wage bills (a major part of their costs), they would of course just not be taken seriously. Firms which ignore their costs do not survive.

The costs of employing people who are not at work will fall on the firms which employ them – in this particular case, all firms who employ women (and most do). That is only where they first impact. For what the legislation has done is raise the costs of employing women of child-bearing age relative to the costs of employing men, and women above child-bearing age.

So where will the costs fall? They will fall on young women who want to take jobs. They will find it harder to get jobs, and the jobs they will be offered will pay less than they would have before the legislation. Such women will thus be kept out of the workforce, or pushed into lower-paying activities. As a result of the legislation, women will be discriminated against on the perfectly good grounds that they have suddenly become more expensive.

No government has resources to pay for the benefits they give. In this case the costs fall primarily on women of likely child-bearing age. But the costs do not end there. To prevent entirely rational discrimination against such women (rational discrimination because the government has made them more expensive to employ) laws are passed and enforced to prevent such discrimination. The enforcement of these uses resources, including workers who would otherwise be doing something else, and creates uncertainty among private sector employers.

Extending parental leave to fathers would reduce discrimination against women, but it would also raise the costs of employing all workers. The objective is desirable, but objectives are not rationally sought regardless of cost.

What cheaper ways there are of ensuring that mothers can recover from childbirth and look after their newborns is an interesting and important topic, but would merit at the least a short book. The objective of this 'fallacy exposed' is to show that searching for such cheaper ways would be a good idea.

February 1993
(Updated May 2014)

SOCIAL DUMPING IS A PROBLEM

Some countries in the EC, most recently France when Hoover moved its manufacturing from France to Britain, complain that other countries engage in 'social dumping'. By that they mean that having less restrictive labour legislation, and thus imposing lower costs on business, attracts jobs from one country to another. In an attempt to prevent this, the President of the EC Commission has tried to revive the 'social' part of the EC's plans, so as to prevent such competition.

There are two aspects to this issue. First, is 'social dumping' undesirable? And second, would M. Delors's scheme work? It is useful to take them in order, as the answer to the first bears on the second.

'Social dumping' does harm the countries which lose employment. They have a higher unemployment rate, and a lower level of national income. This happens simply because it is cheaper to do the work elsewhere. The other country (or countries) of course gain. Jobs are gained; output is gained; and income per head is higher.

The last is important. It happens because the size of the population does not go up, but the proportion of it which can work does. There is, in other words, clear gain for the country which gains the jobs.

What would happen if within some set of countries, 'social dumping' were prohibited? The effect would be to impoverish the whole area. Those in work *might* have better conditions – but recollect that output per head of population would be lower, so that countries as a whole would be worse off.

It might seem attractive to deal with the resulting unemployment by imposing tariff barriers – particularly against goods which had previously been produced domestically and were now imported. If these were high enough, they would re-direct production. But it would be high-cost production producing high-cost goods. The workforce might be increased – but wages would buy less.

The basic point, of course, is that we cannot get something for nothing. It may seem appealing to have a 'social charter' for workers. But that is not costless. The cost falls on the whole of society, including most notably those whom a desire to help workers drives out of work.

April 1993

WITH POPULATION GROWTH CONTINUING, IT WILL BE HARDER AND HARDER TO FIND JOBS FOR EVERYONE

There was once a fear that population growth would outstrip the growth of the world's food supply. The consequence was said to be that starvation would eventually constrain the size of the world's population. Thomas Malthus is often, not altogether fairly, identified with this 'Malthusian' doctrine. For the moment that fear has faded. Certainly one factor in that has been the growth in the EU of 'food mountains' – clear proof that if you pay enough, more will be produced.

A modern variant of this fear is that the supply of jobs is limited, and will inevitably be outstripped by the number of those wanting to find work. Occasionally governments in recent years have acted in part on the prompting of these fears. The French government, for example, has given incentives to firms to reduce hours worked per worker so as to increase numbers of workers employed. (The immediate cause of their action may well have been France's persistently high unemployment rate; but the notion of a permanent 'jobs shortage' certainly helped.)

Notice first that there is some measure of inconsistency between the so-called 'Malthusian' fear and the fear of a job shortage. The former implies that there are no limits to what people will consume. The latter implies that there are limits.

Showing that the belief in a permanent jobs shortage is fallacious is best done in two stages.

First, note what happens when any individual gets richer. In all but a tiny minority of ascetics, that individual consumes more. Not necessarily more of the same thing, although more pairs of shoes or more shirts, for example, may well be bought. What happens as an individual gets richer is that a bigger range of goods and services is consumed. Man has an infinite capacity for discovery, and this capacity is not limited to the discovery of new medicines. As the centuries have passed people have consumed more varieties of clothes, carpets, foods, books, and entertainments. The habit of going to theatres and concerts developed. The cinema was invented, the television, the record player, and so forth. The steam engine and the motor car replaced the horse as a means of transport – although (a good illustration of a point made below) the horse continued to be used in leisure activities.

The time may yet come when mankind is sated with consumption – but it has not come yet, and shows no signs of doing so. On those grounds alone, there is no reason for believing that there will be no jobs for a growing population. That population will, on the evidence so far available, find work producing increasing varieties of goods to be consumed.

But the argument that there is no danger of a long-run shortage of jobs does not end there. Suppose people do start to consume a smaller fraction of income. This means inevitably, as a matter of arithmetic, that a larger fraction of it is saved. Rising savings will tend to lower rates of interest and, in turn, to encourage investment. If capital is used increasingly relative to labour in the production of goods, the earnings of labour will be pulled up. This will have two effects – living standards will rise and, a consequence of that, working hours will fall. Leisure is something people like to consume. They will consume more of it, and engage increasingly in time-consuming leisure activities. Note, as mentioned above, the survival of the horse for use in leisure activities, and the growth in the popularity of golf, a prodigiously time-consuming sport.

To summarise so far then, a rising population will not encounter a fixed number of jobs. First, because this rising population will itself want to consume. Second, because technical progress (which shows no signs of slowing) will lead to the production of an ever-expanding range of consumer goods. And third, because as the earnings of labour rise, people will wish to consume more leisure. All these have occurred over the past centuries. (Not necessarily at a steady rate, of course; working hours, for example, have floated up and down, but about a falling trend.) The forces which have ensured that jobs have been available in the past for an ever-expanding population are all rooted in mankind's desires to consume and to enjoy leisure. So long as these fundamental human motives remain jobs will be created.

Of course this does not mean that there will never be an unemployment problem. There can be temporary fluctuations in unemployment, related to the business cycle. And unemployment can be created by well-intended but ill-designed social legislation. But there will never be a permanent shortage of jobs unless human nature undergoes a fundamental change.

March 1997

IMPOSING LABOUR STANDARDS HELPS THE
POOR AND PROTECTS DOMESTIC WORKERS

Firms that produce goods in developing countries and sell them in developed countries have recently been attacked from two points of view. They are blamed for the low wages their workers receive; and they are blamed for causing unemployment in developed countries, by importing goods which undercut domestic producers. One problem with such arguments is that they neglect comparative advantage: if countries can produce goods relatively cheaply because they have abundant labour, then objecting to imports of their goods is like objecting to imports of gold from countries which have gold mines.

But the focus of this 'fallacy exposed' is different. The aim is to show that it is possible to help workers abroad or protect firms at home but it is *not possible to do both* just by requiring higher labour standards abroad.

If the industry abroad is competitive, then workers at home are helped. And if the industry is not competitive, but rather the firm is the main or only employer of labour in that industry, then one can help the employees in the developing countries, but higher labour standards are of no benefit to firms in the developed country. These two points are shown in that order.

Suppose there are two industries in the developing country, one producing 'tradables', the other 'non-tradables'. Both industries are competitive; workers therefore are paid the value of what they produce, and workers are free to move between industries so they earn the same in both industries. Now impose 'higher labour standards' on the tradable industry. This raises the cost of labour, so fewer workers are employed. The industry produces fewer goods, so the price rises, and the competing firms (and their workers) in the developed economy are helped. But what about the developing economy?

First, the workers displaced from the tradable sector go to work in the non-tradable sector, reducing the earnings of workers there. Further, since the supply of goods produced has gone down, the earnings of everyone involved in that sector fall. And the bad news does not end there. The developing economy has been made less efficient. Labour resources are now more useful in one sector than in another. But they cannot move to take advantage of that, because of the 'labour standards'.

Now what about the case where the tradable sector in the developing country is a single firm? Here imposing higher labour standards – up to a certain limit – does not cause unemployment. Why not? Because previously every worker the employer took on added more to his wage bill than just the worker's wages. The reason is that, to attract any additional worker, he had to pay the additional worker more; but every worker had to get the same wages, so they *all* got more.

Now, however, in effect a minimum is set by the labour standards. Up to a certain number of workers, an additional worker costs the same, so no more is added to labour costs when they are taken on than the wage they are paid. So imposing the standard need not raise the price of the good by reducing the supply of it. What it does is raise the earnings of the workers in the tradable industry, and that is all.

So in this case, the workers in the developing country are helped, but there is no effect in the developed country.

To conclude, imposing higher labour standards in developing countries might help workers there – but it is at least as likely, indeed probably more likely, to harm them. And only in that case are workers and industries in the developed world helped.

March 2002

WORKERS SHOULD HOLD SHARES IN
THE COMPANY THEY WORK FOR

It has become fashionable to urge that workers should invest in the shares of the firm for which they work. This, it is claimed, will better align the interests of workers and shareholders, and make for more harmonious industrial relations while also raising productivity.

But the idea misunderstands the nature of the contract between workers and firms. Further, to urge that workers buy shares in their employer is to neglect a significant risk. Meanwhile, an opportunity to advance a related plan which would be beneficial to the working of the economy is being neglected.

Even without owning shares in their employer, workers and employers have interests in common. In particular, they all benefit from the survival, and indeed prosperity, of the firm. Suppose the firm goes out of business. Shareholders obviously suffer, but so do the employees. The latter suffer in two ways. First, they have to find other jobs. This is costly. Whether or not financial expenditure is involved, valuable time and effort both certainly are. Another cost relates to the new jobs the workers eventually find. Skills are seldom perfectly transferable. Being a check-out assistant for one firm will involve somewhat different procedures from doing the job at another firm. Those moving with 'professional' skills have to apply them in a new environment, with new colleagues.

All workers therefore have an interest in the prosperity of the firm for which they work. Should they own shares in it, the interest is of course increased. But this increase comes at a risk, highlighted by the recent failure of Enron. Many workers for that firm had a large part, sometimes even all, of their savings invested in it. They thus lost savings just at a time when they most wanted them.

This is plainly bad from the workers' point of view, and it could also have harmful spillover effects. That the workers as well as the shareholders were suffering would undoubtedly increase pressure for the failed firm to be bailed out with taxpayers' money. This in turn both wastes resources – the taxpayers would otherwise be investing in firms which were sufficiently useful as to be capable of surviving – and provides a marginal encouragement to imprudent management.

There is, however, a related proposal which would improve efficiency, and is being neglected. Again Enron provides an example. Lower-level workers lost their savings because their holdings of Enron shares were locked into their pension funds. Senior management, meanwhile, although perhaps having some of their Enron shares in their pension funds also held many of them in their 'tradable' share portfolios. They could, and in some cases did, sell them.

The example of Enron is (on the available evidence) rather special. But suppose we were dealing with a firm where management was not so instinctively risk-loving. Think of the effect it would have if senior management were required to hold their entire pension fund in the company's shares. If the company failed (or when it did badly) their pension fund would suffer. For this to be really effective as an incentive, pension contracts for senior management would have to be re-written, so that the risk associated with the pension lay with the prospective pensioners. So, to be effective, we would require senior management pensions to be defined contribution, and invested completely in the company's shares.

The proposal is flexible. It would be possible, and perfectly reasonable, for the proportion of the pensions invested in the firm's shares to fall as one moved towards more and more junior management. And indeed, if it were so wished, the proportion not invested in the company's shares could provide a defined benefit pension.

It might be objected that the scheme involves too much interference in the working of firms. But, at least in the financial sector, where the long-term stability of firms is particularly important, there is substantial interference already.

So to conclude. Urging worker ownership of their employer's shares both neglects that workers and employers' interests are aligned without that, and forgets the substantial additional risks such shareholding brings. There is, however, a case where the additional risk could be beneficial. If senior management were locked into the shares of the company they managed, they would undoubtedly pay heed to the long-term interests of the company.

June 2002

ABOUT THE IEA

The Institute is a research and educational charity (No. CC 235 351), limited by guarantee. Its mission is to improve understanding of the fundamental institutions of a free society by analysing and expounding the role of markets in solving economic and social problems.

The IEA achieves its mission by:

- a high-quality publishing programme
- conferences, seminars, lectures and other events
- outreach to school and college students
- brokering media introductions and appearances

The IEA, which was established in 1955 by the late Sir Antony Fisher, is an educational charity, not a political organisation. It is independent of any political party or group and does not carry on activities intended to affect support for any political party or candidate in any election or referendum, or at any other time. It is financed by sales of publications, conference fees and voluntary donations.

In addition to its main series of publications the IEA also publishes a quarterly journal, *Economic Affairs*.

The IEA is aided in its work by a distinguished international Academic Advisory Council and an eminent panel of Honorary Fellows. Together with other academics, they review prospective IEA publications, their comments being passed on anonymously to authors. All IEA papers are therefore subject to the same rigorous independent refereeing process as used by leading academic journals.

IEA publications enjoy widespread classroom use and course adoptions in schools and universities. They are also sold throughout the world and often translated/reprinted.

Since 1974 the IEA has helped to create a worldwide network of 100 similar institutions in over 70 countries. They are all independent but share the IEA's mission.

Views expressed in the IEA's publications are those of the authors, not those of the Institute (which has no corporate view), its Managing Trustees, Academic Advisory Council members or senior staff.

Members of the Institute's Academic Advisory Council, Honorary Fellows, Trustees and Staff are listed on the following page.

The Institute gratefully acknowledges financial support for its publications programme and other work from a generous benefaction by the late Alec and Beryl Warren.

The Institute of Economic Affairs
2 Lord North Street, Westminster, London SW1P 3LB
Tel: 020 7799 8900
Fax: 020 7799 2137
Email: iea@iea.org.uk
Internet: iea.org.uk

Other papers recently published by the IEA include:

Does Britain Need a Financial Regulator?
Statutory Regulation, Private Regulation and Financial Markets
Terry Arthur & Philip Booth
Hobart Paper 169; ISBN 978-0-255-36593-2; £12.50

Hayek's The Constitution of Liberty
An Account of Its Argument
Eugene F. Miller
Occasional Paper 144; ISBN 978-0-255-36637-3; £12.50

Fair Trade Without the Froth
A Dispassionate Economic Analysis of 'Fair Trade'
Sushil Mohan
Hobart Paper 170; ISBN 978-0-255-36645-8; £10.00

A New Understanding of Poverty
Poverty Measurement and Policy Implications
Kristian Niemietz
Research Monograph 65; ISBN 978-0-255-36638-0; £12.50

The Challenge of Immigration
A Radical Solution
Gary S. Becker
Occasional Paper 145; ISBN 978-0-255-36613-7; £7.50

Sharper Axes, Lower Taxes
Big Steps to a Smaller State
Edited by Philip Booth
Hobart Paperback 38; ISBN 978-0-255-36648-9; £12.50

Self-employment, Small Firms and Enterprise
Peter Urwin
Research Monograph 66; ISBN 978-0-255-36610-6; £12.50

Crises of Governments
The Ongoing Global Financial Crisis and Recession
Robert Barro
Occasional Paper 146; ISBN 978-0-255-36657-1; £7.50

… and the Pursuit of Happiness
Wellbeing and the Role of Government
Edited by Philip Booth
Readings 64; ISBN 978-0-255-36656-4; £12.50

Public Choice – A Primer
Eamonn Butler
Occasional Paper 147; ISBN 978-0-255-36650-2; £10.00

The Profit Motive in Education: Continuing the Revolution
Edited by James B. Stanfield
Readings 65; ISBN 978-0-255-36646-5; £12.50

Which Road Ahead – Government or Market?
Oliver Knipping & Richard Wellings
Hobart Paper 171; ISBN 978-0-255-36619-9; £10.00

The Future of the Commons
Beyond Market Failure and Government Regulation
Elinor Ostrom et al.
Occasional Paper 148; ISBN 978-0-255-36653-3; £10.00

Redefining the Poverty Debate
Why a War on Markets Is No Substitute for a War on Poverty
Kristian Niemietz
Research Monograph 67; ISBN 978-0-255-36652-6; £12.50

The Euro – the Beginning, the Middle … and the End?
Edited by Philip Booth
Hobart Paperback 39; ISBN 978-0-255-36680-9; £12.50

The Shadow Economy
Friedrich Schneider & Colin C. Williams
Hobart Paper 172; ISBN 978-0-255-36674-8; £12.50

Quack Policy
Abusing Science in the Cause of Paternalism
Jamie Whyte
Hobart Paper 173; ISBN 978-0-255-36673-1; £10.00

Foundations of a Free Society
Eamonn Butler
Occasional Paper 149; ISBN 978-0-255-36687-8; £12.50

The Government Debt Iceberg
Jagadeesh Gokhale
Research Monograph 68; ISBN 978-0-255-36666-3; £10.00

A U-Turn on the Road to Serfdom
Grover Norquist
Occasional Paper 150; ISBN 978-0-255-36686-1; £10.00

New Private Monies – A Bit-Part Player?
Kevin Dowd
Hobart Paper 174; ISBN 978-0-255-36694-6; £10.00

From Crisis to Confidence – Macroeconomics after the Crash
Roger Koppl
Hobart Paper 175; ISBN 978-0-255-36693-9; £12.50

Other IEA publications

Comprehensive information on other publications and the wider work of the IEA can be found at www.iea.org.uk. To order any publication please see below.

Personal customers

Orders from personal customers should be directed to the IEA:

Clare Rusbridge
IEA
2 Lord North Street
FREEPOST LON10168
London SW1P 3YZ
Tel: 020 7799 8907. Fax: 020 7799 2137
Email: sales@iea.org.uk

Trade customers

All orders from the book trade should be directed to the IEA's distributor:

NBN International (IEA Orders)
Orders Dept.
NBN International
10 Thornbury Road
Plymouth PL6 7PP
Tel: 01752 202301, Fax: 01752 202333
Email: orders@nbninternational.com

IEA subscriptions

The IEA also offers a subscription service to its publications. For a single annual payment (currently £42.00 in the UK), subscribers receive every monograph the IEA publishes. For more information please contact:

Clare Rusbridge
Subscriptions
IEA
2 Lord North Street
FREEPOST LON10168
London SW1P 3YZ
Tel: 020 7799 8907, Fax: 020 7799 2137
Email: crusbridge@iea.org.uk